We Poked a Hole in The Wind

D1707462

WE POKED A HOLE IN THE WIND

The Story of Two Old Codgers
Fulfilling a Dream

by

Loyal McCammond

We Poked a Hole in The Wind

All Rights Reserved © 2011 by Loyal McCammond

Book design by Robert T. Garcia, Garcia Publishing Services / www.gpsdesign.net.
Background Cover Photo Copyright © Robert T. Garcia.
Interior Photos, Cover Author photo, and Back Cover Author Photo: : Copyright © Loyal McCammond.

 Published in 2011 by
JADA Press
Jacksonville, FL

JADA

ISBN: 978-0-9843558-8-4

Printed in the United States of America

When Bert mentioned that we should write a book about our trail ride, I told him. "Let's get started." Bert got out his old manual typewriter and put a new ribbon on it and started his rendition of our story. But before we really got started putting it together Bert succumbed to cancer.

He was so inspirational in the thoughts penned in this book. Matter of fact, Bert was the reason the task was finished. On his death bed he knew that he was going to pass at any time and the most important thing to him was that I make a promise to him that I would finish writing about the trail ride and share our adventure with everyone. His last request to me was to "make sure you tell it all." I hope that with the help of the mighty hand of our Creator I have done just so. Unfortunately, Bert passed away before this book could be compiled, edited and published, but I'm sure that he would have been pleased to know that this book finally got to the publishers to be printed.

When I started to finalize the first edition of this book, I was faced with the choice of making it first person, present tense or past tense. For a writer, with very little writing and/or prose experience, I had trouble making a choice. Finally I figured that if I told this through the eyes of Bert that the whole world would know him better. So, it is with the greatest respect and admiration that I now offer this book with such a special dedication to my dear friend, Bert Lefevre.

DEDICATION

There were many who said this trip could never be made. We made it because we are both dreamers. So it would only be right that this book be dedicated first to the dreamers out there who have wanted to do something all their lives. If two old codgers, with very limited means, can make a trip like this, then this is a story that you can use to make your dream come true.

Secondly, we would like to dedicate this book to our wives and loved ones who were so supportive of our dreams.

We would also like to dedicate the book to the folks who loaned us the equipment and the animals to make this trip and those who helped us haul the stock back to California for us.

PREFACE

You are about to experience an adventure during which a 50-year-old and a 70-year-old cross part of four states, 700 plus miles and three major deserts on horseback with no support system.

With three mules, two horses, two set of panniers, and a destination in mind two "Old Codgers" set out on horseback across parts of four states and three major deserts to fulfill a dream. As Loyal states in the book this was the most challenging thing both physically and mentally, that he has ever dealt with. This book has a way of letting you share the trials and tribulations that Bert and Loyal encountered.

The author tells what it was like to travel across country the way folks traveled a hundred and fifty years ago. Anyone who has ever dreamed of sharing such an adventure will enjoy reading this book.

First Day on the Trail

CHAPTER ONE

W ell! There we were, sitting at that moment high above Antelope Lake in Plumas County, California, atop the Sierra Nevada Range. We were on our trek to Glenns Ferry, Idaho. From our vantage point on top, which might have made an eagle turn green with envy, we could look down and see Antelope Lake far below. Although the sun was shining brightly, there were clouds above and below us, and there was definitely a chill in the air. Even with that, our animals were wet with sweat and all lathered up. Those last four miles were straight up, or so it had seemed to us.

Actually, it was all uphill and very, very steep in places, rough with deer ruts and washouts from the recent rains and melting snow. It was sure enough hard going for tired out and heavily laden animals such as ours.

Each time we would stop to let them rest and get their wind back, they would sigh and seem to say, "My God, ain't we ever gonna get there?" Little did they know what lay ahead. And that went for us, too. I wonder, would we maybe have changed our minds if we could have looked ahead.

No, no, hell no! It could never happen. We're just too damn tough, see. We kept telling ourselves this until I think we finally got to believing it ourselves. But now, I wonder if perhaps a word other than "tough" might have been more appropriate.

However, what we had just come through was almost indescribable, Too beautiful for words. Timber you just wouldn't believe. And this is coming from an old lumberjack who had acquired the notion that all the good timber had already been cut. Not so. There's really magnificent Ponderosa (yellow pine), huge sugar pine, all kinds of fir and cedar, and *Christmas* trees (mostly white fir) on the mountain sides by the millions.

And every place the good Lord saw fit to put a meadow, he did. The wild grasses were lush and green, with just about every color of green there is, I reckon. One thing I know for sure. It'll take a man a lot smarter than me to fully describe how it really works. And another thing I'm fairly sure of is that it won't be much longer and "Big Money" will gobble it up so quick that it'll make your head swim.

Now we're back on the trail again and whoa, whoa! It looks as though Loyal and that damned red mule are having another go round, the way the mule, O.D., was stepping about, as tired as he was. Loyal's face is still scabbed over from their last go round. The reason for this fiasco seems to be that a big four-point buck and three does had just stepped onto the road and they seemed to be really interested in what Loyal and O.D. were up to. I couldn't speak for the mule, of course, but Loyal seemed to be doing just fine. He had O.D.'s lead rope dallied up so tight around his saddle horn that the bugger could hardly breathe. And I was quite sure it was about over. The big brown mule Loyal was riding at that moment was a big enough mule and strong enough to hold about anything he'd dallied to. He sure was a tough old bugger. I had to give him that.

We were well on our way to Wemple's cabin. At this altitude we knew it couldn't be too far. We'd never seen the cabin. We had only heard about it. But it looked as though it may have been all down hill from there on in. We sure hoped so. I didn't know if our dog Buck was going to be able to follow us or not, and I sure hoped we weren't going to have to carry him. Well, we found out real soon that we were going to have to make some alternate plans for the dog.

So, finally, we came around a bend in the mountain road and there stood Wemple's Cabin and some much needed rest. That was our destination for the day when we left my nephew's place in North Arm that morning. It seemed like it had been a week ago, and it had only been twenty-five plus miles? Hard to believe. Well, I guess we had asked for it, and we made it.

The Two-Holer.

CHAPTER TWO

Wemple's cabin was an old pioneer's cabin and a historical landmark, and it sure looked good to us. My nephew and a friend had stayed here on a deer hunting trip some time ago. It was everything he said it was and then some, particularly for the animals. There was lots of good grass to graze the animals on and a stream running right through the property. There was even an old pole corral, but it was not in the best of shape. The gate was long since missing, but we figured we could put some work into it and it would hold the stock for a while. The cabin was a one-room building with a corrugated metal roof and one-inch plank sides. The wood had weathered with age and looked like it had been burned to get its color, but that's the way old wood in this area looks after many years. It had a good plank-wood floor. The two windows were long gone and the door was hanging by just one hinge. The cabin was clean with two good metal army bunks, believe it or not. An old wood stove was set up in what was probably the kitchen area. It hadn't been used in years. So that left us to plan on using our trusted Coleman two-burner stove. We unloaded the stock of all the packs and saddles right outside the cabin door and led the stock over by the corral. We then started shoring up the sides of the round corral. Then with a long pole we constructed a makeshift gate. Then we led the animals into the corral and turned them loose.

The first thing they did was roll and shake. By now the sweat and salt on their hides was probably starting to bother them. We both discussed the need to take them down to the stream in the morning and give them a good rinsing off. We gave them the last of the grain we had been packing. They ate it as if it was their last meal. They walked around the corral a few times then all of them bedded down for a good rest.

Someone (vandals) had torn the door off the outhouse. Now mind you, this was a two-holer. This pioneer family must have been quite well off to afford the luxuries of a two-holer.

Needless to say, Loyal got the door and put it back in place and then he walked off and took a good look and said, "That's the way she should look."

All I could think was, *how could you argue with that?*

It was getting dark outside, and we'd been going strong since daybreak. We still had to get unpacked, get out the food and the two-burner Coleman stove, and get ready for bed. Then maybe I could take time to write a little bit. That day was the first chance I've had, since we started, to write anything. And then I made a big mistake.

I said, "Are we having fun yet, Loyal?" That did it. He gave me the blackest look I think I'd ever seen, grabbed a roll of toilet paper and headed for the outhouse. What I didn't know until later was that he had taken some pain pills to help him with his constant pain and it had really tore up his system from one end to the other, literally.

I thought he must have gone to sleep out there; he was still out there after I had done the chores that needed to be done to get supper on the road. I had also packed in a bucket of water to wash and to cook with. It took quite a bit of time just going through all our gear to find the things needed to put together a full meal. I decided right then and there that we had to get better organized with those packs.

I had to step outside and call Loyal not once but twice for supper. When he did come in, he explained the pill situation and I then understood what had happened. After a good supper, such as it was, he made up his bunk and turned in. Sleeping bag and a sack of clothes for a pillow, and he was soon fast asleep. I got busy writing by candle light and in longhand (of course). If I'd taken a typewriter it would have been smashed to smithereens long before we got to Wemple's cabin. Well, I finally went to bed too, and I think I dozed off for a very short time. It seemed like a half hour or so. It must have been longer `cause it was getting light outside and oh boy was it ever cold! .

"Jesus Ke-rist, Loyal," I blurted. "It's cold in here. You got the coffee made yet?"

"Hell no," he says, "I've been waiting for you to make it."

"Well, I'll be damned if I'm going to lie here and freeze to death." I said.

So I made him happy and got up and made coffee pretty quickly. Then I said, to no one in particular, like maybe I was talking to the dog, "By God, this is just about the best cup of coffee I've ever thrown a lip over. Nope, you can't have any, Buck; there wouldn't be any for Loyal if I give you some. Reckon I should have made more, cause this is about gone already."

That did it, there came Loyal like a big bear, only the bear's got a coffee cup in his paw.

"Well," I went on, "there's ice all over outside, but the sky's clear, so before long the sun will be in here and it'll warm up. Everything will be just fine."

"I'll tell you what I'll do, Loyal," says I, "I'll get breakfast and do the dishes afterwards if you take care of the animals, okay?"

"Sure," he says back.

CHAPTER THREE

Just in case you all are wondering why, how, and what for we got on top of this mountain range, I'm about to tell you. Well, the *what for* is easy, like the chicken crossing the road. We wanted to get to the other side. Had to, as a matter of fact. The *how* is a little more complicated, having to do with horses and mules (maybe one sort of bad mule), and the weather. Personally, I don't think O.D., our big red beautiful mule, wanted to come along with us anyway, but how do you ask a mule? You can't just say, "Hey, old buddy, want to come along with us?" And then, we get around to *why*? Why have we come as far as we have on the way to wherever we're going? The reasons are many and run the gamut from weak, puny, senseless, to and through irresponsible, ridiculous, and down right stupid. I prefer irrepressible urge, commitment (having to do with my honor), and/or just plain going to do it anyway come hell or high water. So right or wrong we don't give a damn; we're going to do it anyway. I reckon we both figured the best way was just to throw a pack on O.D. and light out. Oh, and one thing for sure was that we had treated him a helluva lot better than he's treated us so far. So there.

This all probably started a couple years ago when my brother-in-law Verd came down from Glenns Ferry, Idaho, to visit us at our home in Paradise, California. Verd and his new wife Sherrie insisted that we visit them and see their new home. I knew that my wife, Jan, having lung problems, wouldn't go. Because of her health problem, traveling was a thing of the past.

"Verd," I said, "I've been meaning to buy me a horse and saddle, and take a little ride up and see you all. How do you like that?"

"Well," he said, "I'd like that just fine; you do that." Now, I know for sure as I was setting there, he thinks that I was full of B.S. So I made my mind up then and there to take care of that little chore. And meant to do it if I lived long enough.

I don't know if it started then, or if it was on Thanksgiving Day when my wife's sister Rosie visited us with her brand-new hubby, Loyal. Yep! This was Loyal and the first time I'd ever seen him. During the course of our visit, I just happened to mention the fact that I'm going to buy a saddle horse and take a little ride to Glenns Ferry, Idaho, on the Snake River. Loyal kind of smiled at me and said, "Let's go but we probably can't go until late next spring."

He then started reaching for his back pocket. He pulled out his billfold and took a tattered piece of paper out and handed it to me. It was creased from the folds but on it was a list of items needed to make a long horseback trail ride. Loyal had been planning one of these long trail rides for years and years. He said he had made several week or ten-day ones but this sounded like the challenge he was after. Loyal said he thought he knew where he could get a couple of horses and a couple of mules and his cousin Wayne had the pack saddles we could borrow. Loyal said, "What do you think about that?"

Well, about that time I'm thinking that we should run Loyal for president or something. Not only was he full of good ideas, he's also (evidently) had most everything else we'd need for the journey. So, before I dropped a block of wood on my foot or something else, like getting caught with my mouth wide open, as it was then, I figured I'd better say something . . . "On account of the weather?"

"No," he says, "because we'll have to get some animals in shape."

He says that we should be able to get out of here by the 1st of May. If we need more time we can wait until sometime in June, but we need to be across the deserts before it gets too hot. Believe me, this was not the last time that Loyal's knowledge of trail riding would come in handy. Then I told him I was going to buy my own horse and would start looking right away.

Sitting on the floor next to my guitar amplifier were two coffee cans, one two-pound and one three-pound, into which I'd been putting all my spare change for quite a spell. By last count there was about six hundred bucks in there and I thought that if I was careful and lucky there was my horse and saddle that I was going to be riding to Idaho.

Before we turned into bed that night, Loyal said, "I'll figure it's a deal then, okay?"

I said, "Ole Buddy, we've got ourselves a deal, and you can bet your socks on that, and not to figure running around barefoot either!"

Bert's Morgan Mare

CHAPTER FOUR

G ood night. I'm not sure this story started even then, because there was so much work to be done, and so little time to do it in and, of course, Loyal was in the same predicament as I was. He had some packing equipment but not nearly enough to make a long trek across four states on a long pack trip. Loyal left and went home to the Fiddletown area to start gathering the stock and the rest of the tack for this trip. The mules and young horse he planned on taking needed to be worked and worked and worked. He talked one of his neighbors into taking their young Arab gelding on the trip. Loyal had told him that if the young horse did make the trip he would be one whale of a horse when he came back. He also borrowed three mules from his cousin Wayne.

He also borrowed a whole bunch of tack as well as the panniers from his cousin Wayne.

He spent all fall, winter and spring riding and packing this pack string, trying to get them in good shape. Needless to say, to get his posterior in shape also. He would ride and pack them several times a week up and down the Consumnes River area and then take off into the wilderness up above Fiddletown, California, with his stock loaded for a long trip. Training three mules and an Arab gelding was quite a chore. But he'd done it before and knew what had to be done prior to putting out on a long ride. He stopped graining the stock and made them graze for their food. This made them able to survive areas where we would not be able to carry or get horse feed for them.

Now this turned out to be a particularly wet, cold, and thoroughly miserable winter and spring. To sort of round out the whole situation, let's just throw in twenty-two inches of snow, and the wind that broke off or blew down about half the trees on this piece of property. All of this kept me as busy as the proverbial three-toed cat, cutting wood and piling and burning brush. As yet, I didn't have a place for the horse that I still hadn't gotten, but I was sure in there trying (are you keeping up with me?). However, Loyal said he'd bring me up a load of fence posts from his place in Fiddletown. As they have lots of cedar and lodge pole pine, that'll be just the right size for what we want.

And on top of everything else there was to do,

my landlady asked if I could make a place for her forty-five-foot trailer house. She had been paying one hundred and fifty dollars a month space rental in a trailer park. She decided not to rent it out again since she had to evict the last two tenants when they stopped paying their rent.

"Well, good old Bert," I said, "Why sure, don't worry about a thing, I'll take care of it."

So, brushing out a road, pulling stumps, leveling out and graveling a pad, tearing down the trailer, and moving it (hell 'twasn't nothing) kept me really busy. Everybody knows I just love working in the rain, the mud and the snow (like hell I do). You must know by now, I really like my landlady or I wouldn't have done it. I hope she reads this. Maybe she'll buy a book.

And, all that time I'm thinking about my horse. There were a few horses advertised in the local paper and I'd looked at some of them. But there was this little Arab-Morgan mare that had caught my eye, and she hadn't been handled or ridden for about four years, so they told me. It took quite awhile to catch her, but Loyal is a whiz-bang around horses, and pretty soon he came down the hill leading her by the tongue. I'll tell you, it didn't take long to get her attention. I didn't buy her right then, as I didn't like the price near as well as I liked the horse. They wanted five hundred, then four fifty, then next time four hundred. I went back two or three weeks later, and probably four or five bales of oat and alfalfa hay later (at ten bucks a bale). I guess the guy was tired of looking at me or maybe feeding her. So he asked how much I'd give him for the horse then and there.

"Well," I said, "I'll give you two hundred for her right this minute."

He said, "Fork it over."

I had to leave her there a couple days, till I could get a fence to hold her. Then when I came back I bought her a saddle and bridle for one hundred dollars from the same people. We put up the fence in just one day; about one hundred by one hundred and twenty-five feet, using the posts that Loyal had brought up, and barbed wire I bought on sale in Chico. Since we didn't anticipate any problems with the mare fence-wise, we felt fairly confident that we were at least making headway with our plans and rode her home that day.

Loyal had brought along his own saddle because it fit him so good and because he said, "If I'm going to have to educate that mare on the way home, I'd just as leave have my own saddle because it'll take a whole bunch of her pitchin' to unseat me. I don't want to blame you for buying an old hundred dollar one."

Anyway, as my old Grandad would have said, he rode her home. Once she found out who was boss (and of course it was Loyal), she settled down and brought him home in a hurry. Turned out to be a very good and very reliable saddle-horse.

Well, back to the rain and the snow and the mud

and all the other little goodies that were fast becoming an important part of our sojourn. Oh yes, and let's not forget about that dirty little four-letter word "work." After about two more weeks of the above, here comes Loyal with a big horse trailer holding three mules, a horse, and what looked like enough tack and whatever else it took to make a real long pack trip . . . His landlord in Fiddletown was so curious as to how two (what seemed to be) sane men were going to pull this trip off that he volunteered to haul the whole kit and caboodle up to Paradise. He was still shaking his head when he started back down the hill home back to Fiddletown.

It didn't take long to get acquainted with Buford, the big brown jack mule that Loyal had been riding for sometime. Then there was a sorrel colored mule named O.D., a spoiled rotten young mule who needed an attitude adjustment according to Loyal.

Next was Honey, a little molly mule (and I mean little) about the size of a big burro, a regular little doll. She was never a bit of trouble the whole trip. Because she had to trot to keep up with the rest of us, her little feet just twinkled on the trail and I would get so sleepy watching them that I actually had trouble staying awake. Last of all there was Duke, a regular gentleman of a horse. He was a registered Arabian, a very gentle five-year-old gelding who, because of his loving disposition, became a nuisance at times. We never had to tie him up or hobble him because he just would not leave people. But on the trail he was as fast a walker as I believe I have ever seen. My little mare was a fast walker also, although Duke's runnin' walk covered more ground. I think Loyal had to keep him in that gait or he'd slow down; he certainly pulled his weight on the whole trip. They were all a really good bunch of animals for this ride and a whole hell of a lot better than we had a few months ago.

Finally, it kind of seemed as though everything was coming together, like maybe it's supposed to happen this way. Another thing seemed strange to me, like I told Loyal a whole bunch of times. It seemed I'd done or seen most all of this before, like; nothing seemed to surprise me. Some funny feeling, by golly. Well, son of a gun, just weeks from being seventy years old and I'd never quite realized all of this before. "Time marches on." Or "How time flies." Or "Boy, time just drags on, doesn't it?" I guess I always figured these axioms were just filler-ins for speech patterns when folks couldn't think of anything to say really quick and didn't want to take the chance of getting in an argument. But, alas, here comes the first of May barreling down on us like it said in the old country song about the train called "Old 97" with old Pete the engineer sitting there with one hand on the throttle and the other one on the whistle, coming down the grade like a bat out of hell and all that's on his mind is time. The last thing they said to him was get her in on time. Well, I reckon time and old Pete really did fly and they're still going somewhere; and for sure, that is the by golliest truth you ever read about.

I sure did have to hand it to Loyal, though. He was here a week before the first of May and raring to go. However, he didn't get much past the coffee pot and the kitchen table. When they were first getting out of their pickup it started to rain and rain and rain. It was just the way it happened. We figured the best way to handle that was the way they do in Texas, just let it rain.

We managed to work with the animals every day, since they were still really rough. Raining or not they had to learn about hobbles and ropes and good manners. Loyal had made some long trail rides in the past and I sure was glad because all this was all new to me. I sometimes thought maybe the animals were getting the best of us, you know, the upper hand. They were teaching me quite a bit, but Loyal said, "Hell, we put shoes on them buggers, and they didn't put any on us, did they?"

I had to admit he was right. But, every bit of new experience we gained along the way helped us to be ready for the unknown we would encounter further down the trail. After a couple weeks of "mudding" it, Loyal went back home for a while, after agreeing the first of June would be better for all concerned. We would leave then regardless of the weather. If we left any later, we risked getting out on the desert at a time of year when we might not be able to find water to keep us going. Here we are now up to our drawers in water, but all the same, we had three deserts to cross and one of them the Black Rock Desert. By our guesstimate it was about one hundred miles across.

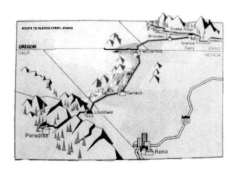

Route to Glenns Ferry.

CHAPTER FIVE

Loyal had bought some topographic (TOPO) maps that covered the eastern part of California and some very good maps to cross the northwest part of Nevada with. One of the most widely used of all maps is the topographic map. The feature that most distinguishes topographic maps from maps of other types is the use of contour lines to portray the shape and elevation of the land. Topographic maps render the three-dimensional ups and downs of the terrain on a two-dimensional surface. Not knowing where we would cross the southwest part of Idaho all we had was a common road map of Idaho.

We had laid three maps out on the dining room table and we drew a line with a three-foot ruler and ball point pen from point A to point B. A was Paradise, California. B was Glenns Ferry, Idaho. That was the way we planned to go; hardly a single road. We knew we wanted to avoid all public roads, and this is where the TOPO maps of the Forest Service would come in handy. Folks, I'm here to tell y`all we underestimated the southwest corner of Idaho.

I'd noticed that when someone asked Loyal when, where and why we were going, he'd turn away and leave the answer to me. I'd pretend I didn't hear either and get really busy doing something whether it needed doing or not.

But when Loyal did answer, that's if they got him point blank face to face and he didn't have any way to avoid answering, he'd only say, "Well, we just want to go look at the Snake River as soon as we can."

He allowed that answered all three questions. Now, I never knew him to tell a lie, not any more than I would, but if he was telling the truth then, and I believe he was, he sure wanted to see that Snake River powerful bad.

CHAPTER SIX

The morning of our start we got our muddy duds off, showered and put a new change of clothes on. We swung up in our saddles and I leaned out of the saddle and gave my wife her last kiss (for a little while) and away we went, slogging through the mud. Snake River here we come. I'll never forget the morning we left my house. It was ten thirty and we went one mile cross country to line up with an old abandoned railroad grade left over from the old days. That suited our purpose just fine. All we wanted was a safe way to get through town and this was as near as we could get to that. On this little cross country jaunt was an old concrete bridge, hardly safe I'm sure. It was about ten feet wide, no sides on it and covered with litter. What else could you call it but a slab. Loyal and

I had crossed it several times on the big mule and my mare and we didn't figure on a problem with them. But as for the other animals, we didn't know. When we got there, Loyal was ridin' the old brown mule Buford and he just dallied up the lead rope on O.D., the red mule, tight around his saddle horn; and he said he even threw a hooey (whatever that is), and across they went. He didn't mess with O.D. one bit and just started across, period. O.D. didn't want to go. However, he went backwards and sideways but across just the same. The others followed really easy. I reckon they saw what happened to O.D. and wanted none of that. The first hurdle and a good start for a good trip, just keeping our fingers crossed. Pretty quick we were on the track bed and headed up for town.

Just like long ago on a Saturday night when we were young.

Loyal waited for me at the old depot, while I rode down to the feed store, where I had some very good friends who I had promised to let know when we were taking off. They jumped in their cars and came up to take pictures of our little string. Every block or two the town streets crossed the old rail bed, and they would be there taking pictures. Kind of made us feel better as we were getting off. I had strapped on my pistol, my thirty-thirty was in its scabbard, and my old cowboy hat was pushed back. "Hell, man," I thought, "this is living."

Now my wife had called the local newspaper

office a few days before and told them we, Bert Lefevre and Loyal McCammond, were going on a horseback ride with pack mules to Idaho.

The girl in the newspaper office said, and I'll quote her, "Well that's fine, I hope they have a nice trip. Tell them to call us when they get back."

So, I tell you now, it did feel good to have at least a few people to see us off. And, off we went, fire in the hole, and ready to take on the whole world. I sure was hoping the water would still be out there for the animals to drink further down the trail.

On account of too much brush on the railroad bed we crossed the highway at Magalia and rode up through town, crossed the highway again to Coutelenc Road back onto the right of way as far as we could go. Then on up Doons Grade and after a while back to the highway, where we crossed the Skyway at the Lovelock Inn and, oh man how I wanted to stop for a beer. I've always been a very reliable beer drinker, and I sure wanted a beer mighty bad.

But I'd told Loyal, "Hell, no beer drinking ain't going to bother me any."

I should have added that not drinking is going to be the hurting part of all this. But, as either I have or have not said, my word is my bond. But, Katy, beautiful Katy, who owns the Lovelock Inn is a very special friend of mine and not stopping had a very sobering effect on me, Savvy? I may live through it anyway.

We've got two miles to go, all uphill, and then

we'll be home for the night at the old corral. We had driven up here in the car and checked this old corral out. It had been an old homestead. Across the road was an old apple orchard. Just up the road was the remains of a very small cemetery. We had a loading chute and two small corrals, one to hold the stock in and one for us to bed down in. We could also keep our equipment secure that way. Because this was the first day of riding, I think Loyal was looking forward to this as much as I was.

A month or so previous to our leaving, I had answered an ad in the local paper about a dog some people were trying to give away. It was a border collie and I decided to take him along with us even though Loyal tried every which way to convince me he shouldn't come. He told me of many dogs who couldn't make one of his long trail rides (I'm stubborn too). He was only nine months old, a good-looking dog, and he became part of our trip. He didn't know anything to do but run because we did not have much time to train him; he immediately became a problem the day we left. We were sort of skeptical about leading him through town because our pack animals were not completely broken in and might not go along with that. They could stampede through somebody's house, wreck a car, or worse.

"Simple," my wife said, "why can't we take him through town in the car and give him to you out there somewhere?"

My wife and Loyal's wife certainly did not approve of this trip, not even a little bit. I thought they figured us to be "too dad burn stubborn" (the way they put it) and were now eager to have us gone. But no, it wasn't that way. The way they cried you'd think they were going to miss not having us underfoot all the time. Well such are love and life, Both are wonderful, I reckon. They met us with the dog on the other side of town and brought each of us a drink and a hamburger. All the while they were arguing with us to change our plans. To please turn around and come home. And, they would have told you that we were the stubborn ones (Ain't it funny what makes women have that kind of protectiveness for what's theirs). My old Granddad was surely right about no man being able to figure out a woman.

Well, the women had made up their minds to try one more time to change our minds, I reckon, cause about half a mile out from where we were going, they pulled up behind us. We didn't mind one bit since they had a big bucket full of fried chicken and all the trimmings.

I immediately volunteered to get supper and do the dishes, though Loyal insisted too. So I packed up some water from the small stream running along the edge of the pasture and made some coffee. We built up a good fire and had a very nice evening. The girls stayed with us until just before dark, then said their goodbyes and drove off down Powellton Road. So went day one and you can tell I was tired.

Camped in Humbug Valley.

CHAPTER SEVEN

All too soon it was morning again and are we ready? You can bet your boots we are; either that or we're both awfully good at pretending. This morning proved to us we could make it on the trail. We couldn't go inside to rest and have a cup of coffee. We had none of the luxuries we had enjoyed back home. Folks, this was for real. Make a body think of the theme to *Rawhide—Get 'em up...move 'em out...*or something to that effect.

We started out on the old Powellton Road and then hit the upper part of the Skyway just south of Inskip. This was an old hotel that used to be quite active in the gold mining days, and when the logging industry was quite active it served as a hotel/café and, well, I'll let you guess. The little café was still open for the few loggers who occasionally came through. Now, I told you about going past the Lovelock Tavern without getting a beer.

Well, it was Loyal who said, "Bert, it's a long way to Glenns Ferry." Nuff' said. Oh, how ice cold that beer was.

We only figured to make Snag Lake that day, which would have made it a fair amount of miles to cover in two days. When we rounded the curve, what a beautiful sight Snag Lake was. Snag Lake was a dammed-up fork of the Feather River. It was crystal clear and the water over the spill way was really cold. We looked everywhere for a place to set up camp. But no, not a place big enough off the road to hobble the stock and no corral to put them in. So, we kept going, because it started to cloud up and didn't look too good. On further up Humbug Road on the way to Humbug Summit it started to snow; we put our slickers on and did what they did in Texas. We just pulled that J.B. (J.B. Stetson) down tight on our heads and just kept right on going.

When we reached the summit it was cold and misting snow and Loyal said we could stop here but we're liable to wake up in the morning with everything covered with snow. Now mind you it's in June, but then again we're crossing the Pacific Crest Trail high in the Sierra Nevada Mountains. Loyal said according to the map we had a clearing several miles on down the eastern slope of the mountain. That slope took us all afternoon and then into the evening. Finally right at dark we wound up in Humbug Valley and chose an old cabin with a great gaping hole in the roof. It had a really good corral and lots of good grass for the stock. Glass and all kinds of litter covered the floor of the place, so we kicked enough stuff out of the way to put our canvas tarps down and then put our bed rolls on top of them. Where we had spent last night, on Powellton Road, was like a beautiful picnic ground compared to this place. I truly believe my wife would have thrown up her arms and fainted dead away, could she have seen me and Loyal trying to clear out a place on that filthy floor.

When she came to, she would have said, "You're not going to sleep in that filth, are you? If you do, don't ever plan on ever sleeping with me again. Do you hear me? When you get to Idaho just keep right on going. Don't dare come home."

Now, I want it clearly understood we didn't pick out this place. It was all there was, and it was dark when we got there.

"We can't see in the dark, can we, Loyal?" So we just had to make the best of it. Before we get too much further down the road, we'll have slept in worse places than this one. We'll have bunked with big pack rats, alive and dead, stinking old sheep hides drying on a fence outside the hole where the windows were supposed to be, and, oh my God the flies, those big bloated blue flies. It' s almost too horrible to put on paper. Why did our creator ever get involved with them anyway? Well, they say every cloud has a silver lining, right? So I decided to try and put some silver lining in this one,

"Hey, Loyal," I said. "We made about forty miles today, How does that grab you? Sign down the road says only twelve miles to Lake Almanor. We rest up a little and then we'll be over at my nephew Joe's after one more go around."

"Well," Loyal says, "let's make that a couple of days. We're trying to go too fast and that's the quickest way to slow down."

He was right again, you know, and we spent several hours mucking out this cabin (that's trying to clean it up) and we had to be careful it didn't collapse on us or tip over the way it was leaning. I'm glad we took time to clean it out. Looking out the gaping hole in the roof that night at the stars, I'd never seen them look so pretty and bright. I guess I'd just never paid attention before. Maybe, I'd just never been this tired before. Maybe that's what it was.

But, let me tell you a little more about what happened, earlier, the day before and this morning, when we were loading the packs. It's about a stud horse, running with two others, that kept Loyal on his toes several times during the first day at the valley and the following night. Loyal had anticipated trouble with other horses, and in particular stud horses. So, before we left home, he packed a wrist rocket to bring along for the trip. This is a sling shot that is designed to shoot ball bearings, which it does very well. Loyal is about as close to being an expert with it as you can find, since he's been doing it for years, save for one little thing: when to use it (as we will find out). Loyal had told me to keep my eyes open for some ammo for it, and as luck would have it, I picked up a pound of thirty-eight caliber lead shot at the flea market. It cost me a quarter, and I don't think the people selling it knew what it was. With that we were ready.

The first night we spent at the valley was fine, but the next day a big dappled grey stud found the mare and was trying his damndest to tear down the corral. Loyal went out there soft and easy through the wet grass, sneaking along the fence line 'til he gets exactly where he wants to be, and then, zowie, with that wrist rocket and a ball bearing. I could see he got him really good the first time cause that horse let out a squeal you could hear clear across the valley, giving out enough wind at every jump to carry a balloon on across the Sierras.

Sure beats watching TV and away out here in the boondocks, too. It's amazing. That's what it is. Now that dappled grey would stay away for a while 'til he'd get wind of sweetheart mare, then back he'd come. Loyal was waiting and got him again and again until the horse had to take a rest, which Loyal claimed was just to take on some more air. Now I wonder, what do you think? Well, let me say right now, any threat to the high moral values and the unquestionable integrity of our pack train would be met with Loyal and his fearsome wrist rocket.

So, don't mess with us.

CHAPTER EIGHT

After two nights and a full day's rest, we headed out for Lake Almanor. Only twelve miles and we should be there before noon (HUH?) and probably make another twelve after that (HUH?) and then make it to Joe's early the next morning, and then rest up a day or two . . . you're on the trail with Old Dirty Bert. Didn't you know that? Well now you do, that's for sure.

We started out light-hearted from Humbug Valley all right enough and made about three miles out of it and on up the logging road. That's the only exit to the east, which was the way we were headed. When we were about three miles from where we stayed in Humbug Valley, we stopped to let the horses and mules drink from a rivulet along the side of the road.

Right then Loyal saw a chipmunk on the other side of the creek and immediately went for his weapon, the sling shot.

When that wrist rocket went off in O.D.'s face (so it seemed to him) that mule went straight up and came down bucking for all he was worth, without anyone telling him he didn't have to. The packs slid around under his belly, of course, and were completely emptied. With Buford looking as if he was fixing to start bucking, Loyal turned O.D. loose and down the logging road he went. Loyal brought him back sure enough, but I'm here to tell you that there was never a bigger mess than the one we had to clean up, let alone the damage to the packs and gear.

Before we got going again we took a short breather for ourselves and gave the animals time to settle down a little bit. Man, could I have used a cold beer along about then. I might have just as well been wishing for the moon because I'm out here on a trail across the Sierra Nevada Mountains. Anyone in his right mind would figure by now the damage having been done, and us working so hard to undo it, we'd have a good journey the rest of the day. At least you would think so, wouldn't you? Wishful thinking.

About three miles up the road and about forty-five minutes later, Loyal was on the ground getting a drink of water. I was sitting on my mare, holding Buford and the others, when O.D., the honey mule, and the gelding pulled loose and took off back down the road. Loyal hollered, "I'll get them," and away he rode. Well, he got them turned around, with O.D. trying to buck the pack off. I don't suppose he even knew that Loyal was after him and the other two. So here they came up the road, hell bent for election while there I was afoot on the ground hanging on to Sweetheart's reins. I ran out and positioned myself in front of the other three running animals to stop them, but hell, they went right over the top of me and got tangled up in the reins I was, or rather had been, holding. They ran on past me and about a hundred yards up the road Duke went over an embankment. He was all tangled up and the two mules had stopped and were just milling about on the road.

Loyal ran up hollering, "Are you hurt?"

"I don't know," I said. Anyway, the sorrel was over the bank upside down and couldn't get up. Loyal had to cut the lead rope to get him righted. When he got back to me I was up walking around and feeling places I hadn't felt for a long time.

"I'm all right, I think," I told him. "They probably left tracks on my rear end, up my back, and one shoulder, with an ear skinned up and bleeding, but other than that I'm okay"

"Well, Bert," Loyal said, "In rodeo back in the prairie states where I come from they call that 'being freight-trained.'"

I said, "I'll be damned, here in the middle of nowhere, ain't that something."

Then Loyal added, "Bert, I think somebody up there likes you." And, with that I all of sudden felt a whole lot better. (I could have been killed, you know.) What I wanted to say was, "I'm right at 70 years old; I ain't got no business doing this sort of thing."

Finally, after leaving Humbug Valley, we came to where the road forked; and just to make the day as imperfect as it could get, we took the wrong way and lost a few more miles. We met a fisherman who told us to go back the way we came and stay on the other road, which would bring us to the highway. Finally, we got onto it and headed for Prattville and Lake Almanor.

When we arrived there we tied up and walked across the road to the store. The first thing we got was a couple cans of beer that we had to go outside to drink. The lady inside (the owner, I guess) was making us a couple of sandwiches with real meat (HALLELUJAH). We couldn't tarry too long, as we had to find a place to bed down for the night. We bought a loaf of bread, a couple cans of corned beef, and a couple big cans of beer and were on the road again. Shortly, Loyal spotted a sign that said "P.G.& E. Property, No Admittance."

He looked and said, "Well this is it."

Loyal happened to know that all P.G.& E. property has to have an entrance and egress if it is crossed by a power line. So it didn't take long before we were in a beautiful little meadow with good feed and water and hidden from the highway. We soon had the animals unloaded and Loyal had strung a picket line between two trees and had the animals all tied in a line.

We tried out some of our groceries we had bought earlier and then just as the sun was setting we could see a real beautiful sunset with red and all the colors. Wise mariners know how to interpret the appearance of the sky, and they heed its indications. As a well-known rhyme puts matters: "Red sky at night, sailors' delight; Red sky at morning, sailors take warning."

After the day we had experienced we needed something like this to help us unwind. We were soon in our bedrolls and fast asleep. Everybody and everything happy. Good Night!

CHAPTER NINE

What do you know? It's morning already, early risers. There are stars still in the sky. A cup of coffee, a quick corned beef sandwich, and we're on our way. Too bad we can't fly. We leave the same way we got in, nice and easy, no harm done. P.G.& E., we thank you and I'll think of you every month when I'm paying my gas and electric bills. We had already crossed the spillway at Lake Almanor and were traveling through the small village of Canyon Dam, California, on Highway 89. Then we turned off the highway and headed for the great beyond, east by northeast or as close as we could make it allowing for the rugged terrain and logging roads that went almost everywhere and nowhere (many just ended up at a landing).

Soon it was clear it would be hard to make headway this way, and we decided we'd be better off to back track and follow the highway into Greenville. (We weren't lost. We just didn't know where we were.) My nephew Joe Basham and his family have a ranch on the North Arm of Indian Valley; that is nine miles beyond the town of Greenville on the Diamond Mountain Road. We had intended to cross overland, traveling on the Old Haun Road up through the Old Haun Ranch properties on an old forest service road. Then when we hit the Diamond Mountain Road about three or four miles north of Joe's place we would double back south to where he lives, in the opposite direction from Antelope Lake. The road is the old Stage Coach route.

Anyway, if we go ahead and take the route through Greenville we will come out south of Joe's place. It's the same thing only completely different. Savvy? What they mean when they say it works both ways. We came onto Highway 89 about a mile past Canyon Dam and everything seemed to be working out real fine. Loyal was feeling good (on account of the corned beef, I guess). O.D. was acting real good and I reckoned he had got the meanness out of his system and was going with us of his own accord. All the other animals were doing just about as well as any one could ask for.

My heart was kind of singing along too. Highway 89. The unforgettable Highway 89: very scenic, a trifle crooked, and with narrow shoulders on both sides of the highway. By either hurrying up a little or slowing down a little we were able to keep the roadway open for traffic. Yep! We seemed to have the situation well in hand. I was proud of our little string. They seemed to be completely unconcerned with the traffic whizzing by. Just to be part of all this seemed very important at the moment. There was all sorts of traffic: logging trucks, lumber trucks, cars, vans, and you name it. And then, on a downhill grade some guy with a load of logs, trying to be a good guy, I know, goes to slow down a little bit and lets up on the throttle. That cut in the Jake Brake on the motor, which comes in rumbling and roaring, triggering that (@#%$^^$#) red mule (O.D.), who proceeded to unload his packs right there and then and finish breaking up the rest of our valuables. Right in the middle of Highway 89.

Remember that the panniers, or packs, had been beat up so many times by now that they were mostly bailing wire, barbed wire, nails, screws and spit, with some of that 100 mile an hour grey duct tape holding the whole works together. So up a logging road O.D. goes. He's still got the pack saddle on and the honey mule and gelding are dallied to him, and away goes the lot of them. Loyal, who was riding Buford and was leading the rest of the stock, was stretched out holding the lead rope and got himself bucked off head first into a ditch alongside the road. God, what a bleeding mess he was. An ordinary man would have got himself half killed for sure, and as it was, he didn't miss by far. Before Loyal could even get up, Buford had taken off up the highway. Of course, all the traffic had stopped and the whole highway was full of people, everybody wanting to help. Loyal hated all this.

Loyal yelled, "Watch for Buford and I'll head up after the runaway bunch."

He took off up the logging road after the animals, going as fast as he could go. I had my mare tied up to a tree and was trying to get our junk, yes I said junk, off the highway. I had lots of help, and I told the people that were there to just kick it all in the ditch to clear the road. By now a lady comes down the highway leading Buford, Loyal's mule. I tied him with my mare and then got busy with the gear that was scattered down in the ditch. What was good I carried back across the highway and put in a pile. We had to throw away quite a lot. We lost our horse shoeing equipment: file, nippers, hammer, four half sets of shoes, even what was left of the horse shoe nails. We used some of it to fix the panniers. What the hell, it was all in a day's work . I looked up to where Loyal was coming down an old logging road with the runaways. They had got wound up around a clump of trees and weren't hard to find.

Loyal said, "It wasn't hard to trail them at all. I just followed sugar for a while; then I followed flour; then I followed coffee."

He handed me the lead ropes and I took the run-aways and tied them to a tree beside the mare. Loyal headed down to a creek to wash off some of the blood and to see how badly he was hurt. He didn't really know how bad that was until a couple of days later. He's a tough old bird, that guy. He did say something about how O.D. would make a good candidate for the glue factory. Really, I believe if O.D. was Loyal's mule he would have pulled out the .30-.30 and modified him to the point that O.D. would never cause us any more problems. But of course O.D. is a borrowed mule and in Loyal's care for training, so I reckon this saga of Loyal versus O.D. is not over.

I told Loyal about the pretty lady that brought Buford back, and me being all shook up like Elvis Presley. I couldn't remember whether or not I had thanked her. Loyal said, "Hell, don't worry about her. She got to see the whole damn rodeo what with trick riding and a stampede and she didn't even have to buy a ticket. What is the price of a rodeo ticket these days?" Loyal had blood on his shirt and pants as well as his face, He hardly changed his expression when I informed him that most of his clothes had been scattered up and down the highway with the rest of our stuff.

All he had to say was: "Hell, I'll wait till we get to Joe's. I'll shower, shave and put clean clothes on there. Okay? I think we better put this show on the road if we're going to get there by tonight." I had to agree with him, since time, as we talked about, just keeps right on going. After he'd got the blood off his face and neck and ears, he still looked pretty bad, real bad as a matter of fact. Blood still seeped down from a whole bunch of places. Evidently he had hit the ground with the side of his face and it looked like someone had taken a piece of big grit sandpaper and commenced to drag it across the side of his face. He not only looked bad, he looked terrible. We were to find out later he had a broken hand from the wreck.

I also was wondering if someone in Greenville would wonder what had happened to his face. We sure didn't want the law to start asking questions about two old bums going through their town. I casually mentioned to him that when we got to town we'd have to ride down main street and I'd sort of appreciate it if he'd either ride a little ways ahead of me or behind me. Well, that almost did it. He almost lost his sense of humor. He started cussin' and then he started laughin' and I knew I'd said the right thing. He's quite a man.

CHAPTER TEN

It didn't take all that long for Loyal to load the panniers, and he made sure that O.D. was loaded down just as heavy as he thought possible. I'm here to tell y'all that I know a mule can grunt. Matter of fact the other ones were carrying light loads for the rest of the day.

Loyal said, "Let's get on the road again, only this time we'll go up the mountain."

We'd heard a train pass by and knew we were pretty close to the tracks. We followed them for about two miles, but it made us both very nervous. The terrain was very steep and there would be nowhere to go should a train come along. I'm sure that's when Loyal got the idea of tying O.D. to the tracks and getting behind a tree and watching. I knew he was just kidding,

I think. We followed the tracks for a couple of miles.
It was somewhat scary when we started around a curve
because if a train was coming we had no place to go.
We were either in a cut in the mountain or we were on
a steep grade with no place to go but straight down.
We finally spotted a logging road below and when we
could, we made for it. This road paralleled the highway nearly all the way into town. It's what we call an
off-highway road that the truckers use to haul extra
heavy loads (the more the merrier). Being on it and off
the tracks sure took a load off of our minds.

Finally we got into Greenville. They were having some kind of a celebration there, and the town
was full of people. I reckon they thought we were a
part of it all. I guess we were at that, although not the
way they thought we were. By chance we had come
in just at the end of a local parade. We didn't have a
parade number and I'm sure the organizers had no
idea where we came from. We just fell right in behind
the last exhibit and followed them. Anyway, the
crowd waved and hollered at us. And we waved and
hollered back and kept right on going. I reckon they
are still wondering where those two old codgers came
from. With Loyal in the lead and with blood still oozing from his scraped face, I'm quite sure we did look
like authentic mountain men. But, more than likely
we looked like a pair of saddle tramps.

Out the road north to where it becomes Diamond Mountain road and on to my nephew's place.

Hallelujah: We're going to make it and so we did. Some of Joe's neighbors had stopped by his house and told them about a pack train heading their way and told them not to miss it. Joe, his wife Lilly, and their daughter could hardly believe that it could be us, but they had to come to look. They walked up the road and around the bend about a quarter mile and waited. Then sure enough it was us.

Of course, Joe kept saying, "I knew it was you and Loyal, Uncle Bert, but I thought you were coming in from the other direction."

Next he said, "To tell the truth, I didn't think you'd come at all. I just thought you were blowing off steam."

Now, I had talked to Joe on the phone a week or so ago and Joe had told me he didn't think we could make it; too cold, too much snow, too much mud and rain predicted for a few days. Maybe he just didn't think I could or would. Ho-hum.

All I could say was, "You got any beer, Joe?"

"Damn right," he said, "and just to make sure we don't run out, right after supper we'll go to town and get some more. You know," he continued, "we've still got tomorrow too."

Well now, I reckon that's the most beautiful music I'd ever heard out of Joe. Joe is a musician and song writer but I had never heard him write any song as sweet as his last statement. Take my word for it. This is by far the best he has ever done. Lilly, Joe's

59

beautiful wife, just dug in and cooked us up a real good meal, just as though she'd known we were coming. Loyal got his good hot shower, a good hot meal, and clean clothes, not necessarily in that order, and finished up with a couple of cold beers and a good soft bed. In the morning he told us he thought he'd died and gone to Heaven. He said when his time comes around, and if it's like that, he won't mind a bit.

Well, after supper was over Joe and I went to town to buy some more beer, lots of it. Joe and I sat up most of the night playing our guitars and Joe singing. We had an unforgettable time.

Next morning, Joe had every thing we needed to work with, and before the day was out we had everything fixed up better than when we started out. Loyal said to travel lighter we would have to leave a lot of things we wouldn't need. I mean really need. Like my thirty-thirty rifle, two boxes of ammunition, scabbard, ropes, hobbles, binoculars, extra clothing, coats (not needed on the desert), hunting knives, whetstones, extra tools, a couple of extra blankets. It included all the things I had brought along just in case. We had a scale we were going to use to make sure that we had the panniers of equal weight. Well the scales must have weighed in at about ten pounds, and Loyal said we would have to just lift the panniers and guesstimate the weight. We placed it all in a big pile and we reckoned it was probably 150 pounds. We

would be better off without all that weight. I didn't
part with my side arm and later was sure glad of that.

Loading up at Diamond Mountain.

CHAPTER ELEVEN

We started off the following morning at daybreak planning to make Antelope Lake, twenty-six miles from Joe's place. It was a long way to go, but Joe said if we make that and have time we ought to try for Wemple's cabin. A mighty tall order, right? But anyway, we would sure give it a try, although we might run into snow or the animals might give out. And what if somebody else was in the cabin? Just too bad we couldn't see into the future (just a little). Like I said or maybe haven't said, "What the hell, here goes." And, as you already know, everything has turned out hunky-dory so far.

About two in the afternoon we rode past a place called Brown's cabin. It is located just about three miles west of Antelope Lake. We hesitated and asked each other if we should put up here for the night. It had a roof, a small wooden corral, and a small running stream. What else do you need? With still a lot of sun left we decided to push on. As tired as we were when we arrived at Wemple's cabin that evening, we should have stopped earlier.

Joe just then pulled up in his pickup truck just to see if we'd made it. But he had to leave right away because he had left without taking care of his chores. He sure was worrying about us. Joe had made the trip in a little over two hours, and we had taken all day from sunup to almost sunset. Oh boy, oh boy, oh boy what a day! This is great. I love it. Poor Joe wanted to come with us so bad I thought he was almost on the verge of crying, but he had too many obligations at home. That made me sad too.

Now, we were scheduled to lay over the next day. The day after that my wife and Loyal's wife Rosie were to meet us down the hill in Litchfield to pick up our dog Buck. Buck's feet were just getting worse by the day. Loyal had been on several trail rides in the past and had warned me about taking Buck along. He said that a young dog would run himself to death along the trail. Soon his paws would be raw and he would not be able to make it. Yep! Again he was right. Buck had chased after every sound, critter and/or movement since we started on this journey. We would have tomorrow to rest up, and the day after we would meet them. So, I reckoned everything would be fine as long as we got there on time.

New Shoes for Buford.

CHAPTER TWELVE

When we were about five miles out from Wemple's cabin, I made a terrible discovery. I had either lost my teeth or left them in the cabin: I rode on a little way, thinking it over, and then told Loyal. I'll have to say this, it was the first time I'd seen him grin in three or four days, you know, because it hurt him to grin through his scabs. But, he really did.

"If you want to go back and look for them," he said, "go ahead. But I think I better go on. I told the girls to meet us at about 4 o'clock, and I sure don't want them looking for us."

I said, "Let's go on."

If I were to ride all the way back and not find them, I'd be looking for them all the way down. I was thinking, hell, if I don't find them I'll have to do without anyway. Mostly, what was worrying me was this big bag of beef jerky hanging off my saddle horn. Damn, that's proof positive you can't win them all. I had made about seven pounds of jerky and there's a real good chance I could starve to death. Now, as I've always said, I'm not afraid of dying. I just don't want to be around when it happens. Now, what's worrying me is that if you starve to death don't you have to be there when it happens? Well, of course you do. Worry, worry, worry.

On the other hand, there are far too many things to think about, such as coming down the eastern side of the Sierras, 'specially at this time of year, when all the shrubbery is beginning to show off its fresh bright spring colors. The dew is making everything shine like it's covered with diamonds where the sun sweeps across it. It's incredibly beautiful. You can just sit there on the horse with your arms folded and imagine you're the richest man in the world.

What the hell is money anyway? It's called filthy lucre. Ain't it. And up here you couldn't spend a penny if you had millions of dollars. Ain't that something?

Down in the distance is Honey Lake and the Honey Lake Valley. Sure worth the whole trip just to be able to see it. I'll bet I'm not the first man to ride this old road with no teeth. This is the first road that came through this country. Hacked out by an old

explorer and scout named Noble. It was he who discovered Honey Lake and the Honey Lake Valley in
1851. We were following the same course the old
timers used when they were trying to find an easier
route than the Lassen Trail. We didn't think as we
traveled east northeast that they had traveled west
southwest and probably arrived at their compass
course the same way we did. So, onward and down-
ward if we are to meet our wives at or near the desig-
nated time. We will pass by Honey Lake on our way
to Litchfield which, besides being the meeting place,
is the last place on the map before we enter Nevada.
So it became what we called our jumping off place.
On down off of Janesville grade we crossed US highway 395 and started on a shortcut for Litchfield.

The wives pulled up behind us when we were
about four miles from what we thought then was our
stopping point for the day. We were all surprised by
what we found in Litchfield when we got there: nothing. Well, almost nothing — just a feed store and one
small restaurant (open only in the evening). However,
there were some very nice people who told us of a
ranch where we could spend the night. At the feed
store we finally bought a sack of feed for the animals.
There we met the nice lady who arranged for the
place where we could put our animals up for the
night. We told her we'd be back later for the feed and
whatever else we needed and swung up again and
headed northeast up highway 395 along the side of

the road. The ranch was out about three miles, but quite a place: lots of feed and water for the animals and a good tight fence.

Although we were invited to stay in the big house, we threw down our sleeping bags in an empty tool shed, near where the animals were. Our dog Buck curled up on my sleeping bag, and I could tell he was down for the count. He didn't know about the long ride ahead of him. At least going home with the women, he'd be going in comfort. They brought blankets for him. We'll miss him but sending him back is the only thing to do.

We went back to town and when we got to the restaurant I couldn't hold it any longer (about my teeth). I just had to tell my wife about my teeth before she discovered it herself.

Before I could get started she said to me, "Honey, are your teeth bothering you. You better put them in for dinner."

I told them we'd probably have a nice big steak apiece. And then, the way she smiled, I knew for sure she had found out about my losing them. She had heard Loyal kidding me about not letting him carry the jerky, and I reckon she figured it out from there. I'm not sure if she believed me or not when I told her I'd left them on a rafter in Wemple's cabin. I probably told her Loyal was trying to take the Jerky 'cause he thought I couldn't eat it. I kept right on talking first about one thing, then about the other.

Now, up to this time, she hasn't said a word, and I'm beginning to feel a little bit better about the situation, but I guess she figured it was her turn now, and when she started in nobody had a chance. Like I told everybody, my old daddy was right when he told me years and years ago that no man has ever figured out a woman. He said that if they were to get their heads chopped of their mouths would go right on talking. Well, what do you think? Anybody on my side? No takers?

Anyway, I think they all had a real fine dinner, it sure did look scrumptious. My soft hamburger and bowl of soup was good, too. That's how hungry I was.

The high point of the afternoon was chocolate pie with whipped cream on it. I had been eating kind of slow, but when I saw the waitress bringing some other folks their chocolate pie with whipped cream, I was happier than a flea in a dog pound. I do believe I would have paid one hundred dollars if it had been auctioned off. This was not an evening I would have liked to be playing poker. I wasn't sure if they had got to the last three servings. So I asked if the waitress could bring mine now before everything was gone.

Jan, my wife, still wanted me to take the car and drive back to Wemple's cabin to get my teeth, but I wouldn't do it. I figured after the long ride the girls had already had to pick up the dog, they still had to drive home again. Of course, they were anxious to get away as soon as possible and get home by dark if they could. I figured time was of the essence for them.

Loyal had told the lady down at the feed store that Buford, the big mule, was going to be needing shoes pretty quick; and one of her relatives who had been a mule shoer up at Bishop, California, during all the Mule Days, came over that afternoon with his tools. He shod Buford all the way around and didn't even want pay for it, only the price of the shoes. Loyal wouldn't go for that and he paid him very well. I'm just mentioning this so that you know what kind of people are out there. They're really something else and we found this to be true for the whole trip.

CHAPTER THIRTEEN

Well, by the dawn's early light we were on our way again. Yes! This was our jumpin' off spot. From now on we were destined to travel back roads, cow trails, mountain passes and mainly just wide-open country. After a few miles on Highway 395 northeast of Litchfield we passed the Bureau of Land Management wild horse corrals. Only a short way along, we came to a monument in honor of the aforementioned explorer Noble and his party of 1851. We rested there a short while and then went onward again.

Just a little while up the road a car went by and then stopped and backed up alongside us. I noticed that the license plates on the car were from Kentucky. A man and a woman got out of the car and he introduced himself as a commercial photographer. After chatting awhile, he asked if he could take some pictures of us. We told him sure, go ahead, and he took quite a few while Loyal was fretting about we're burnin' daylight.

The photographer was exuberant and said that they had traveled three thousand miles and these were the kind of pictures that he was hoping to get.

He kept saying, "You sure look authentic."

Finally, I said to him, "Hell, we are authentic, flesh and blood just like you, just traveling is all."

That kind of got him flustered, and he started apologizing. When they finally left he was one happy man. There were four other cars that stopped to see what was going on. Loyal doesn't care for all this attention. He'd rather be off in the brush somewhere.

Another hundred yards down the highway was a gravel road turning off to the right with a cattle guard and a gate nearby in a gully. On the map it was the Smoke Creek Desert Road. The map showed that it took us all the way to where we were to start crossing the Smoke Creek Desert. So away we went, out toward the desert.

We were in sheep country now and there were jackrabbits by the hundreds. The sagebrush was all about one or two feet high, and we could see jackrabbits everywhere we looked. Dead rabbits were all over the place, but strangely there were no buzzards. I mentioned this to Loyal and he said he'd noticed it too. We saw a few ravens (they feed on dead animals also), but no buzzards. I could hardly get over that.

Later we found out why. They'd all been poisoned. Lots of people were using the jack rabbits for target practice and leaving them lie. The sheep men and their hired hands then poisoned them as bait to kill off the coyotes, who live off sheep as well. The buzzards got poisoned too.

It's a cruel world out where the long trail is. I haven't been keeping track of all the animals we've seen on this trip, because we've seen so many of them. Animals in the wild are not afraid of horses. We've seen deer by the dozen, maybe more than that. They just come out in the open to see what's going on and show absolutely no fear of men on horseback. We've also seen coyotes, a zillion ground squirrels and several other critters up to this point. Then there were the prairie dogs at Wemple's cabin. These are not squirrels. These are honest-to-God prairie dogs. I'm at a loss why they were up there so high, but they were.

About an hour and a half out this road, Loyal spotted a windmill. It was turning and seemed to be pumping and there were a few cattle around, which is always a good sign. So we headed up through the rocks toward it, with everything seeming to go as smoothly as we could hope. Then O.D., who had been perfect for a long time up to now, decided he had gone far enough and just set his feet, bringing our party to a halt. Loyal tried pulling him, jerking him this way and that.

I was looking around to see if there was a rattler about when Loyal yelled at me, "Bert, take Buford." He was already off of him and I said to myself, "This is it for O.D." Well, it had been coming for quite awhile.

Loyal said, "Take them over there a little way, might as well get this over with." Just as if he'd said, "Bert, you got any Grey Poupon?" Well, believe it or not, seeing him as calm as he was then, (and I could have been wrong) I didn't think he was a bit mad, so I began to feel better. Maybe he didn't intend to kill O.D. after all. However, out in these lava rocks anything could happen. What if Loyal got jerked down and dragged through these rocks? God almighty, anything could happen.

All this went through my mind in a flash as I took my nine millimeter out of the saddle-bags and got ready for God knows what. I could be a very rich man today if I'd had a camcorder and knew how to use it.

This would be the battle to end all battles. Man against Beast. Loyal started it by pulling on that rope so hard it actually looked like it stretched that mule's neck out about two and a half feet. Finally when the mule couldn't take it anymore he started to buck and rear up on his hind legs. Loyal never gave up an inch of slack, just started backwards kind of feeling his way through the rocks, Jerking that mule's head from one side to the other then up and down. He kept him from rearing up again and was (believe it or not) actually dragging him. When the mule would panic and come at him, he'd belt him on the nose and really jerk him around. This whole operation must have taken ten or fifteen minutes. I don't know exactly. I do know that I was so tired from watching and trying to keep those other animals quiet I lost all track of time. To prove it I would have drunk a whole case of Budweiser, if I'd had it. But, you know, when that mule finally quit, it was all at once, like he knew he was beaten.

When Loyal turned and walked up the hill to the water tank, that mule followed him like a puppy. Loyal had hollered at me to stay where I was. Then he walked back down with O.D., got on Buford, and started back up the hill again, with O.D. following like nothing had happened. 'Twas only then that Loyal got down and rubbed O.D.'s neck and ears and talked to him soft and easy like, as if they'd always been the best of friends. Ain't that something! I'm telling you, I wouldn't have missed this trip for love or money. I said to Loyal a little later that I believed O.D. had learned his lesson and would probably be a lot better mule now, but Loyal shook his head no; and then he said, "We'll see."

I got to thinking along about then, you know something, Loyal's a lot like that mule in many ways. Hard to figure is one, stubborn is two, tough is three, stubborn is four, etc. When we finished our business at the water hole, we shoved off again for wherever we were going. We may or may not have been tired, but we were sure weary; and sometimes that's even worse than being tired (sort of mental, I guess), sort of like it's all mixed together.

Count the holes.

CHAPTER FOURTEEN

Anyway, we camped out at the first place that had grass and water for the stock. By a stroke of luck (bad luck) it happened to be a sheep camp. We were headed down the road a piece, and on our way there, when a car came along with a cowman and family from Nevada on their way home from working sheep all day. They said they had worked and culled and shipped several loads of sheep that day. He had given this sheep ranch to his son and was helping him out a little. Sure we were welcome to stay as long as we would like. Loyal told him one night would be enough. He told us how to get to his place in Nevada. His ranch headquarters was on the north-western edge of the Smoke Creek Desert. Everyone in those parts calls it the "Old Holler Place."

"Well", said Loyal, "we'll be pullin' in there to-morrow evening, I reckon".

The sheep folks had butchered some sheep that day and had left the hides hanging over the fence right outside the bunkhouse door. The windows were all knocked out and the place was full of trash and those big blowflies were everywhere. They are either green or blue, and having already filled up on the bloody sheep hides, they were fixin' to stay the night with us. "The hell with that," Loyal said. "I'll get rid of them just before dark."

I said, "Ok, we'll see."

This beyond a doubt was the filthiest place I'd ever been in in my entire life. I mean it, a pickup load of cans, bottles, and I mean just plain garbage, including all the pots and pans (including the frying pan) all over the floor. Loyal was in the other room and I asked him how it looked.

He said, "Same as yours."

I never even bothered to look. I turned the mattress over, twice, meaning there was no good side anywhere. So I got out the tarp, folded it double, threw my sleeping bag on top, and waited for Loyal to get the damn blowflies out of here. I still hadn't made up my mind to stay in there yet. I lay down just for a minute and looked this place over pretty good. I'm sure enough gonna write about this one. It looked as though someone had sat here on the bed and shot the refrigerator full of holes. I'd say there were some twenty-seven holes in it. Up on the wall hung an old rotten pair of bull-hide chaps. They had probably been hanging there for twenty, thirty, forty years; who knows? They wouldn't hang there much longer, as it turned out.

I was looking at the filth on the floor, for lack of something else to do. When I heard sort of a scraping noise, I looked up and a great big rat, big as a grey squirrel, was coming from a hole in the ceiling. When I moved it scurried under the pair of old chaps hanging there. I didn't want to scare it out because it would just come back later, so I called as softy as I could to Loyal.

He knew something was wrong; he stepped to the door. "What is it?" he said.

"He's under there," and I pointed to the old chaps. He could see the chaps move.

"Goddammit, what's under there?" he said.

I'm pretty sure his hair was standing on end when I told him it was a big rat, big as a grey squirrel.

"Oh," he said, and I could hear the relief in his voice. He picked up an old cast iron fryin' pan off the floor and swung for all he was worth. That fryin' pan was a twelve-incher, and heavy like you wouldn't believe, unless you've used one. Well, he got the rat, he got the chaps, part of the ceiling, and damn near all the partition. You know something? My mind just never seems to quit working. Then I said out loud, "Hell, I don't think it's gonna rain. I think I'll throw my sleeping bag out with the horses, if you don't mind."

Then Loyal said, "It'll be better in the morning."

I couldn't get away from the ugly bloated blowflies, blue or green, fast enough. Couldn't eat, couldn't write, no moving around (too much trash on the floor). I just sat there, didn't want to keep Loyal awake. I guess he was doing the same as I was, just staying awake.

Loyal had gotten rid of the blowflies, but when it started to sprinkle rain, here they came, more than ever. What God put them on this earth for, I'll never know.

Loyal confided in me that he hadn't slept a wink that night, and I think I made it perfectly clear to him I didn't either. So who cares, just glad to get that stinkin' mess behind us.

So tra-la, tra-la. "Loyal, will you pass me the Grey Poupon, please. Thank you, sir."

CHAPTER FIFTEEN

Hurry, Hurry, Hurry. On the way out the next morning we met a bunch of cowboys from the Spanish Springs Ranch. That's the same ranch that John Hamilton advertises on the San Francisco radio station KGO on Saturday morning. Here we get to see our first real cowboys. They were all dolled up in their chinks (a short pair of chaps), flat-topped hats, and wild rags and every one of them was settin' sittin' a big stout horse with a good stock saddle. The man in charge said the hands were from Peru and they made the best cowboys. They all had good cow sense and really were able to take care of the cattle like we have read about in the forming of the great cattle empires of the Old West. They were pushing cattle toward Bull Flats to work them in the corrals there. We know somewhere in that area was the Nevada border. The cowboys told us it was just as we crossed the next creek.

When we crossed Rush Creek we were in Nevada. Hooray! We had left California and were into our second of four states we wanted to cross.

This made Loyal happy. He likes the lonely country, like Nevada. He had been saying right along that when we get into Nevada, then we'll start making some good time. I didn't think we had been doing so badly until now. But the proof is in the pudding, as they say, And I don't know exactly what that means either. I'm more inclined to think, the hurrier we go, the behinder we get. And yep, 'twas Loyal who brought that thought to me. Several times he'd said, "When you try to go too fast, you're gonna lose time." Anyway, any day, I'd rather have a piece of chocolate pie, and Loyal can have all the pudding. So, this is Rush Creek, and if anybody mentions Limbaugh, I'll take a club to whoever says it. This is really good water, almost as cold as ice water, and it just tastes so good. This creek runs right around Burro Mountain. According to our cattleman friend Epsil, there used to be lots of burros as well as wild horses in these parts, but they've been catching them out of here for so long, they're really getting scarce.

We'd wasted too much time talking to the cowboys just west of the state line, so we decided, instead of cooking lunch beside the stream we would settle for a peanut butter and jelly sandwich. I tried to gum some jerky but with no teeth that didn't work. We dumped out and refilled our water bags and canteen. We had hobbled the animals and let them get a few mouths full of grass while we were eating. After we tightened up the cinches again, we were headed down the yellow dirt road, tra-la, tra.-la, tra-la.

This evening will go fast. We'll sleep right through it and in the morning begin a great adventure. We're going to take a crack at the Smoke Creek Desert, against all advice.

Loyal said, "We got mules; nobody ever lost a mule in that desert yet."

There is supposed to be a lake of nearly boiling water, and there sure have been a lot of good people that didn't make it, along with their teams and wagons. There are pot holes, air holes, sink holes, shifting sand, and lots of water under you all the time.

Finally, we got to the cattle ranch. It was neat and clean, even the corrals and barns. It was definitely a well kept ranch. There were a few ranch hands walking about, taking care of things. They were expecting us all right, and one of them came over and introduced himself and told us to put up in the scale house (that's where they weight their stock as they are shipping them to market). They had it cleaned up just for us.

I told Loyal, "Gee whiz, they're treating us like royalty."

"Well," he says, "keep your hand close to your billfold, until we find out for sure."

Well, these fellows brought hay for our stock, checked the water troughs, and made sure we had all the comforts of home. I reckoned they'd had their orders. What a big difference this setting was compared to the son's place we had put up at the night before. After a good hot meal and plenty of coffee, I had nothing to worry about except hitting the sleeping bag and having an affair with the most beautiful girl in the world (the girl of my dreams). Gosh, she was a beauty.

CHAPTER SIXTEEN

I left her there in the morning when we took off to tackle the desert. I said to Loyal, "Which way?"

He said, "See that desert over there? That's us, straight across the middle." Loyal set a straight course for the railroad section house just west of Gerlach (When Loyal sets a course he's bound and determined he'll make it. As I heard someone say one time, "Come hell or high water").

We had made the best part of the flat alkali-looking surface when Loyal turned just a little to the left and we came out just about 1/4 mile from where he had put the dot on the map that morning. About a mile from the railroad tracks we encountered some mushy ground with small pools of water scattered all around.

It took only a little while before my little mare started into a sink hole But with a fantastic leap, one that almost dumped me over her backside because it was unexpected and so quick, she made it out. It sure took the krik out of my back, though; it hasn't bothered me since, but my neck sure hurt for a few days.

Gerlach was straight ahead just off to the east about three miles. We had saved about five hours traveling straight across the flat, Smoke Creek Desert. And we didn't slide into the history books and I'm glad of it. About a mile or so out on the desert from Gerlach was a calving shed. Loyal said, "We can stay here tonight." And so we did.

The next morning we went into Gerlach and found the owner, a Joe Penado, and he said, "Sure, feel free to put up there." He also owned and operated the Jalisco Club. It was the only cafe/beer joint on the west end of town. We had a good meal and a couple of beers and went back to the shed. The next morning just as we had rolled out of our bed rolls we heard a vehicle coming and it was this Joe fella and his pickup was loaded down with hay for our stock. We tried to pay him.

"Absolutely not," he said. "Your stock eat what they want, my cows clean up the rest, okay"

The water from the hot springs was drinkable but very hot. He was telling us it'd be all right to water the horses and mules for a couple of days, and then we would have to pack water to them, because, like his cattle, if they had to drink it more than two days in a row it would make them sick.

"Too many minerals," he said.

He had a small corral and an old cast iron eagle claw leg type bathtub for a water trough. We put the stock inside the corral and after Loyal cleaned and washed the tub out good, I poured several five gallon buckets of water in the tub. Knowing it would take quite some time for it to cool we closed the gate to the corral so the horses couldn't get to the water. As soon as Joe left, we cut across the desert and beat him back to his own club. Matter of fact, I was drinking a beer when he came in. I believe in two days we'd had about everything on his menu. Man oh man, it sure was good. Loyal asked Joe if he knew of anyone around in the Gerlach area who could shoe horses.

He said, "Sure, my best friend Bob Crawford who is the range boss for the Spanish Springs Ranch back on the California/Nevada border."

He called him up and soon he came over to the club and we talked a while. He wanted to look the stock over and shoe them this very night. But we told him we were going to lay over.

So he said, "I'll bring everything I'll be needing to shoe the little Arab gelding."

I want to say this here and now. I've sure had to change my attitude about people, and we weren't just meeting the best of them. They were all like that. We sure appreciated every one of them. The time went by so fast, the biggest drunk in the world wouldn't have had time to get drunk. And I didn't either. This Bob Crawford drove all the way to the next town called Empire to buy us some special shoes he wanted to use on Duke, the little Arab gelding. It was getting dark as he pulled up to start the shoeing, and we finished up using his pickup lights while I was holding a flash-light.

Bob was really upset that anyone had ever put shoes on Duke because he had such hard hooves he probably never would have had to be shod.

Bob wouldn't take a penny for his work, not even, for the shoes he had bought.

CHAPTER SEVENTEEN

The little gelding was ready to go and right after daybreak the next morning we were ready to hit the trail.

After circling through Gerlach, calling the women, and having a good breakfast, we circled to the left on to the Black Rock Desert and were on our way again. Everyone said this was the best way to go. There was a road, such as it was, that took off and went straight across. You could see tracks in the surface of the desert. They were not sunken in like you would find in pasture land. You could tell a vehicle had traveled across the desert. This was where all the auto racing was done.

Starting way back in the 1950s Craig Breedlove had set the world land speed record right on the same path we were traveling across the Black Rock Desert. So that's the way we traveled, straight out. About three hours later we turned right and went straight up the middle of the desert. Our map showed the Quinn River and a Quinn River crossing. That's where we were heading. I don't know why, now, except we figured we'd maybe have to cross the river and this might maybe be the only place to do it. The Quinn river crossing, what a laugh! We joked all the rest of the way about it. What there was amounted to a half dozen potholes for a distance of about thirty feet. Some of them were not even a foot across, just sort of suspended there in the mud and salt. My mare acted like she'd like to cross and I can't say I'd blame her, because there wasn't a damn thing on this side.

On her first step she was in mud up to her knees. I got her out of there fast. Odd things happen on these deserts and I for one ain't taking any chances. Since this is truly a salt desert, the only thing that grew here, and only here around water if it was raining, is a little shrub or brush (perhaps a type of sage brush that I don't recognize). How did we find the Quinn River Crossing? Well, along about four o'clock Loyal began to comment on where we would tie up for the night. We always tied the "bell mare" (folks, that's the animal that is on the top of the pecking order) to a fence post or a tree. Folks, there weren't nary a fence post let alone a tree nowhere, just flat nothing.

Loyal stood up as high as he could in his stirrups

and saw what looked like a fence post off to the north. We headed for it. It was just visible on the horizon. This turned out to be a monument on the National Trail Register. The one thing that made this memorable was a short piece of railroad rail sunk into the salt and probably in cement, with a steel plate welded onto a cross piece about eighteen inches long. It indicated a date, name and purpose. "Noble and party, 1851." This made four of these markers we had come across, enough to tell us that we were traveling the same course set by them, since I believe they came across the Snake River at Glenns Ferry, Idaho. And since that's our destination, I think probably they got their course same as we did: Three maps on the table, a yardstick, a pencil line, and a compass. We traveled opposite directions, ours north by northeast, theirs just the opposite, south by southwest. Too bad. I'd liked to have met them on the trail. Maybe we could have traded them our red mule for something.

Probably the main reason that this trip has been so interesting is the fact that there are so many alternatives. We can do it this way or that way or the right way or the wrong way or we can do it our way. If it comes right down to it we don't have to do it at all. But I think nine out of ten times, we'll do it our way, right? Our wives think we're stubborn. Well, maybe stubborn is the right thing to be, sometimes, don't you reckon? We used Noble's marker to picket the mare. We gave her only a short rope, because there was no feed for any of the animals anyway. We had to be careful how we hobbled the others. They would surely take off if they got the chance. I don't think either of us slept at all. and I know we were both glad when we could get goin' again.

The wind was blowin' fairly hard. I didn't think it'd be quite so hot. It was about 80 degrees yesterday, but I think it's easier to travel in the heat than to face the wind on this salt desert. It wasn't long until the salt begin to build up on our faces and arms. I guess Loyal thought I was laughin' at him and I reckon I was just for a minute.

He said, "What the hell you laughing at?"

I said, "You look so different with all that salt on you."

"Well, look who's talkin'. You don't look so hot yourself." (A good sense of humor comes in handy a whole bunch of times.)

We were heading for a gap in the mountains just to the south of King Lear Peak to the north and east of us. It looked to be about six or seven hours away when we left the Quinn River Crossing. After we had been traveling for about four hours, we realized we still had a long ways to go before getting close to the hills to our east. We didn't want to stop even for a sandwich because these animals were just as hungry as we were, and we owed it to them to get them some food and water as soon as we get off of this salt and into the foothills. If we had had any water we would have washed out their nostrils and squeezed a little water into their mouths. One step after another. It was slow going but we made it.

We were hoping to come out at a windmill on the east edge of the Black Rock Desert. We rode into the sand dunes at the edge of the desert and just as we topped one of the dunes we could see the top of a windmill just to the north of us.

How did they say it, "Eureka"? We felt a little better now, and soon we were riding off to the north to the windmill. It sat just east of a set of car tracks running north and south along the east side of the Black Rock Desert.

Hell with the road, we made a bee-line to the windmill. There was a corral that could be used with a little fixin' up. At the north side of the corral there was an old abandoned line shack. I looked it over pretty good. No one had been in it for a long, long time.

We tied the stock in the corral and then walked very cautiously toward the windmill. Loyal loosened the brake on the windmill, and it took right off, really turning, but nothing happened.

"We're gonna have to prime it," Loyal said.

"With what?" I said. "We don't have but maybe half a canteen of water left. You don't figure on using that, do you?"

Loyal said, "We're gonna have to gamble one way or the other. I'd just as soon do it right here."

I looked at him real hard and said, "You'd better think it over."

Without even changing his tone of voice he just looked up at me and said, "How far are we gonna' get on that little bit of water?"

My god this guy's a talker. Poor Rosie never had a chance. I was thinking it over, real damn good, and I damn near cried as he poured that water down that pump. Nothing happened but a bunch of weird noises. I can still hear them now. Maybe baby ain't coming home, Jan. Maybe baby ain't coming home.

We sat there like a couple of baboons, just waiting. So, I said, "Whata we do now?"

Loyal, just calm and easy like, said, "Well, I guess we'll just go find some water."

"Any ideas?" I said.

"Well," he said, "someone has drove up and down this road, and I reckon there's a reason. They've probably got cattle up there. Lets go see. And right up there is the gap in the mountains we've been heading for all day, so lets go. If there's cattle trails and cow poop, there's water. Take my word for it."

We had planned on going up the western front of the Jackson Mountains. Not too sure where we would ever find water, we were forced to turn in an easterly direction and follow the cow tracks and cow poop. We had ridden about an hour when we saw a big bunch of cows and calves milling around a couple of big water tanks. Just to the east of the tanks was a cliff and out of the cliff was about a two-inch pipe running with a small stream of cold spring water.

We stopped a distance back from the tanks and Loyal had me hold the stock while he went to investigate the best way to water them. He said we should be careful and not let them have too much too soon. He would take two at a time to the tank to let them take a few drinks and then keep rotating them until they were finished drinking. I'll have to admit that Loyal and I got our drinks first.

After the stock had been watered we looked at our map and it looked like we could reach a mining claim called Fish Pond Springs by going through what looked like a crevice in the mountains. After a short ways we picked up a very small running stream and after fighting our way through a lot of small brush and sapling trees and climbing up a very steep grade, we came out in a small valley. This would not be the first time that Ole' Buford the mule would come in handy. He just lowered his head and we came through the brush and timber. It must have sounded like a herd of elephants because we were knocking down small trees and bending some pretty heavy brush. Our legs were bruised somewhat from the beating they took, but we came out the other end. Off to the right was an old mining claim. There were two small buildings and an overhead structure for lowering and lifting heavy machinery down into the mine shaft. Just off to the north of the buildings were two small ponds that were fed by this same spring. It looked like they had been dug out to make holding ponds for the running stream we had come up along as we had climbed up out of the desert. Do you really suppose that someone had the foresight to make these ponds to hold fish, knowing that if they had plenty of water and plenty of fish they could stay there forever if the end came to this system of things? Makes a body wonder, don't it. At least we know now how it got its name, Fish Pond Spring.)

Around the spring was a good bit of good grass for the animals, so they were staked and hobbled and immediately started to devour the green groceries they hadn't seen in quite some time. A big sign, painted in red over the door of one of the buildings, proclaimed this was the Red Scorpion Mine and was the property of the Hem Company of Winnemucca, Nevada.

We set up housekeeping in one of the buildings, and I decided it was time to break out the treat I had been saving for a special occasion. I opened our one can of bacon, got the powdered milk out and made two, not just one but two, go-rounds of white gravy and pan biscuits and crisp fried bacon that two hungry men could eat. Loyal even got up and washed the dishes in the running stream. This was living. Loyal made a special note of this place. He said, "If the world gets too complicated down there in the cities, this would be the best place he could think of to come and live off the land."

Fish Pond Springs.

CHAPTER EIGHTEEN

After two days of Rest and Recuperation, it was time to go. This had been so enjoyable here we both hated to leave. Like I've said before, a man's gotta do what a man's gotta do. We rode out on the road that came to this little hideaway, and soon it ran into another and soon there were roads running all over the place. We just headed out the way we wanted to go, noticing all the new mining claim markers. They were all over the place. We could tell something was going on but didn't know what. We didn't see one person all the time we were there. Strange (We were to find our a little later what this was all about). For the time being we kept on going uphill, higher and higher until we came to the top of this mountain range. There were lots of horse signs.

We were to find out later, there were lots of wild horses and burros in this area.

When we got to where we could look down, we were amazed at what we saw. It was a great broad valley, miles and miles across. The floor of this valley seemed to be covered with alfalfa, which indeed it was. The map showed this to be De Long's Wells. It was far below us because we were a long way up. It looked as though it might take a long time to descend into the valley. It did take us a long time, slippin' and slidin'.

I told Loyal, "The horses and mules won't have a hair left on their butts by the time we get to level ground."

"We'll get down all right," he said. "Don't know what kind of shape we'll be in but we'll get down."

It took us about an hour to ride into the De Long Ranch once we were down into the valley. The De Long family arrived just as we swung down from our mounts. They had been moving cattle from one mountain pasture to another. They were sure glad to see us. They said they didn't get many visitors that came off the desert and crossed the Jackson Mountains. They offered to put us up and feed us. Finally Loyal convinced them that we were burnin' daylight and would be best to go on, and then they insisted we stay at his brother's ranch six miles down the road. I reckon they don't get many visitors. This seemed to be a major event to them. We told them we'd stop and say hello to his brother and family, and that seemed to satisfy them. I reckoned as soon as we left, they made a phone call because everyone seemed to be awaiting our arrival. I guess they really don't get many visitors and acted as if they'd never seen a pack train before.

Loyal said, "They probably haven't ever seen the old antique rigs we're settin'." Loyal was settin' on an old S.C. Gallop saddle with an A fork and a real high back cantle. It dates back to the 1880s. S. C. Gallop is the saddle maker who taught J. T. Frazier how to make all those saddles in Pueblo, Colorado. I told Loyal, "Maybe they think we're out of the past, the 1800's. Maybe we got lost and are just finding our way back."

I guess we look enough like that for it to be true. As we rode up the road in a northerly direction, we passed a ranch on the east side of the road that said De Long on the mail box; but with still at least an hour of daylight Loyal decided we should move on.

Just as the sun was starting to drop over the Jackson Mountains on our left, we approached a ranch that looked as if they might have some corrals we could keep the stock in for the night. We found a lady with two young boys and an older woman tending some cows in the feed lot. We asked if we could put up in their corrals and they said to go ahead. They showed us a good spot on the south side of the feed lot. The older woman came back in a four-wheeled

ATV that she called her red mule, with a couple bales of prairie hay for the stock. Loyal tried to trade her his red mule O.D. for her red mule made by Kawasaki, but she wasn't interested. We unpacked and scattered the hay in a large corral with a big watering trough, and the animals were eating like there was no tomorrow. By now it was just getting dark and we started to figure out just how we were going to eat our peanut butter and jelly this evening when we heard a car pull into the driveway. In just a couple of moments a man approached us and invited us in to eat supper with them. Now, folks, it sure didn't take any kind of persuading whatsoever for us to accept the invitation.

By the time we had exchanged pleasantries and told them a little about our adventure, his wife called us to the supper table. Antelope steak and all the trimmings. Yep! A feast fit for a king. We were served a light green colored drink that really looked like Kool Ade and was real tasty. But to this day I'll never forget the embarrassed look on the Mom's face when one of the boys asked his mom if he could have some more of that "Tidy Bowl" drink. After we had visited a while in the living room the Mom asked us if we would care for some dessert. Of course we would like some. After being on a long trail ride and eating our own cooking and suffering through too many peanut butter and jelly concoctions, I'm here to tell you we were served peach ice cream. Yes, the Swann man even makes deliveries out in the middle of nowhere.

The folks where we stayed told us of a good pumping windmill about twenty-five miles up the road that we might want to stay at the next night. They described how we could find it real easy. They also told us the town of McDermitt was seventy-five miles up that road and they could make it in a couple of hours by car. Now mind you, after a very fine visit with the good folks, I'm sure enjoyed by all, we took advantage of the time that was left and turned in for a few hours' sleep.

CHAPTER NINETEEN

Then up and at 'em again early the next morning. We figured we should be able to make that windmill by mid-afternoon. Just as we were headed out of the corral our hosts kinda threw a kink in our plans when they all at once decided they wanted to take some pictures of us and our outfit. And could we please wait just a little while in the morning until the sun got up. She'd make extra coffee, and we could have all we wanted.

"Sure, Hell yes," I said. "Wouldn't have it any other way." The sun didn't take too long to give them enough light to get a few pictures of us and our stock.

After promising to come back with our wives for a visit (Hell, I wasn't even sure Loyal and I would make it through), we took off and were on our merry way again. We had promised their boy Tommy we'd make a pass around the driveway of his school with the pack string, as he liked to call it, so he could show it to the other kids.

And so we said goodbye to the Willow Creek ranch. As we lined out on the road, I asked Loyal how he liked being a celebrity; and he just grunted. He couldn't care less.

Several miles up road north we came to the school on the left. Sure enough it was a rural school. Mind you, it was not a one-room school; but it was one of the very few "one-teacher schools" left in Nevada.

Later in the day we started looking for the windmill but didn't find it. After a time we decided we'd gone by it or somebody had moved it. So we kept right on going and going like the Energizer bunny again. Soon we came to a big, beautiful concrete bridge and a great big sign saying "Quinn River." I rode down through the river bed and up the other side. It was dry as a bone. The Quinn River at that point hadn't had water in it for quite some time. I wished I knew what was going on.

We left the highway a little farther on. Off to the right we could see what looked like an old gas station. We got up on the hill and swung down. We found out it was an Indian establishment that evidently had been closed long enough for someone to steal all the doors, trusses, and windows from the buildings.

Off to the northeast was a road heading in the direction we knew we needed to be going. Loyal took off across country through the sagebrush with the pack string, and we finally settled down heading north on what looked like a fairly well-traveled road. In a short while we saw a car coming from the north. Loyal flagged them down and he swung down and talked to the folks in the car for quite a while. When he was done he came back to where I was and said the people in the car had told him there was a wind-mill up the road just a short piece. We were on our way again.

Sure enough, in about two miles and just as we turned the bend, we saw a windmill with a huge tank off to the right about two hundred yards. The elusive BLM (Bureau of land Management) windmill. We found out later that it was known as the Radar Well. There it stood majestically turning with a small stream of water coming from the pipe into a tank about thirty feet away.

Loyal took care of the animals while I started getting supper. He washed and curried each animal and then hobbled them and by then supper was ready. Just as the sun was setting in the west, Loyal went into the tank to wash some of the Black Rock Desert off of him. He said it was so refreshing.

There is something about lying in your bedroll listening to the windmill's blades whirling in the wind and the unique sound of the water falling into the tank. Hilton Hotels sure couldn't match this.

When you're crossing country without much water, it's kind of hard to leave a windmill with plenty of water; but we needed to press on.

Back up on the Coyote Point Road we headed north toward a community we thought was The Kings River Ranch. About noon we came upon a small group of houses and trailer houses. To the side of one of the trailers one of the ranch hands was digging a new leach line for his septic system. Loyal said he reckoned we could help, but he was not really too akin to digging. He figured we should push on after we had visited with the man for a spell. The man was sure enough inquisitive as to our reason for the trip and was interested in our equipment. I reckon it's all this old tack and Loyal's saddle. Here was another beautiful green valley surrounded by arid mountain and sagebrush. I figure they pumped all of the irrigation water out of the subsurface of the Kings River. Remember the dry river bed downstream about twenty miles?

On up the pass along a blacktopped highway and off to the left was a rock formation called Sentinel Rock. We left the highway and started a course directly for McDermitt, Nevada. We crossed a small stream running alongside a boundary fence. We unpacked all our gear and hung the saddles and such on the fence and hobbled the animals on the other side. That way they could be close but we didn't have to worry about them getting into our supplies. We stayed just east of Sentinel Rock that night on this babbling little creek that had really good water. This Sentinel Rock is in the old history books. And back in the days of cowboys and Indians this peak was known far and wide as an Indian lookout from the top. They could see for miles and could spot dust a day away in any direction.

I casually mentioned to Loyal, him being retired from the U.S. Army and all, if he'd been around here about 125 years ago his hair might have been hanging from some Indian's belt.

He gave me an odd look and said, "What did you bring that up for. That's exactly what I was thinking about. Was I talking out loud?"

Except for the coyotes howling all night and once or twice my mare, who was picketed on a thirty foot rope and a foot hobble, calling the others to get back here, I slept. But just kinda spotty, I reckon. I had my sleeping bag pointed the right way, and I kept one eye on the top of that rock all night long. That 9 mm under my pillow helped a little, I think. But all I could dream of was Loyal's hair. It's black and real curly. Hell, them Indians would be fighting among themselves over that.

Break Time.

CHAPTER TWENTY

With our hair still on our heads we pulled out real early that morning, knowing it would be a long, hard day into McDermitt. We didn't have a good map but Loyal had set a course for the northeast, hoping we would come out somewhere just south of McDermitt on some highway. For a long time that morning we rode across open range and then we crossed the Quinn River again. This time it was still dryer than a bone. We bypassed an old historical point, Canon Station, off to our south. Loyal said it would mean a half day's ride and we might have to make a dry camp out in the middle of nowhere. We hit highway 95 about twelve miles south of McDermitt. Up the road another few miles we saw a sign telling us we were now entering the Fort McDermitt Indian Reservation.

When you have been riding over open country, it is sad to see the trash and litter you see in the ditches along our highways. We both decided that if Nevada had the pride they should have they would have some of their prisoners out in the ditches policing all the litter. Not knowing what may lie ahead of us and not having good maps, we decided to get a motel in Mcdermott. Besides, Loyal said he needed a good shave and shower. Loyal found a fenced pen just west of the motel and there were a couple bales of feed left over from whoever had used the pen before. So the animals were tended to and seemed to settle down for a good feed and rest.

Resting and relaxing in air-conditioning was quite a change. It gave me a short time to try to write and catch up on our journey. Both of us were able to remember some of the names and places we had encountered in the last few days. With our age we suffer from more that just old muscles.

We tidied ourselves up and went next door to the Casino/Café to enjoy a good meal. Knowing we might be out on the open range for quite a spell, we both ordered a hefty meal. Just as we were finishing up, a man came over and picked up the check. It was the feller Loyal had talked to yesterday digging the septic line.

He said, "I'm buying your supper just cause I want to."

Well, he didn't get an argument from us. All we

could do was thank him. Of course, the last thing he said as he left was that he thought we were "nuts."

We asked the bartender if he knew anyone who might know this back country, as we intended to cross it with horses and mules. He said he'd try to get hold of someone he knew, but how could he get in touch with us.

I told him we were in room 29 in the motel next door. "We're on the back side because the animals were in a pen back there."

CHAPTER TWENTY-ONE

The next morning Loyal went across the street to do our laundry, and I was working on my papers in the motel room. I was kinda hoping Loyal would get done soon so we could go eat. We hadn't had breakfast yet. There came a knock on the door, and thinking it was Loyal with his hands full, I hurried to open the door. At the door was a stranger. He appeared to be a Native American. He looked to be about 40 years old and neatly dressed.

"Are you the guys that are going to cross the Owyhee with a pack train?" he said.

I had to reach back and pick up my vibrator before I could talk. "Come in," I said, "you've got the right place."

The look of surprise quickly left his face, and

when I pulled out a couple of beers I knew we'd be friends. I told him, "My partner Loyal will be back anytime now and I want him to hear what you have to tell us."

"Okay, sure," he said. "It'll take some time, but I've got lots of that ." So he and I just chewed the fat and drank beer until Loyal got there (It took Loyal a little longer to do the laundry than I'd figured. He probably had to run them through twice to get the Black Rock Desert dust and the smell off them).

When Loyal came in I introduced him to my friend. "Loyal, I'd like you to meet my new friend Glenn Able. And Glenn this is Loyal McCammond."

Glenn told us he was a stock contractor for local rodeos. He was also a building contractor and he was born and raised in the Star Valley area, thirty-five miles east of here. That's where we'd be heading in the morning.

Loyal had brought a few groceries with him, and I got out some cheese and sliced off some slabs and passed it around. I think we got all the information we needed including a map (which I still have) hand drawn by Glenn Able. He said he had to go to a funeral at the other reservation, and would stop by the Star Valley Ranch day after tomorrow and see how things were going with us.

We went to the restaurant that evening and had dinner and breakfast combined, so we wouldn't have to take time out in the morning to eat. We would just pack up and go. We'd take care of everything else this evening, like rolling our extra clothes and packing supplies we had bought and all those other little things that needed doing.

Jack's Creek line shack.

CHAPTER TWENTY-TWO

A little apprehensive, but more than a little eager, we cast off for who knows where, or what. Well, we'd find out soon, I reckon.

So far we had had some pretty good TOPO maps, but all we had was a road map to get us across the corner of Oregon and into the southwest corner of Idaho to the highway just south of the Snake River.

Just getting out of McDermott was challenging. We had to backtrack to get to where we wanted to go. We went down an old road that circled out of the southwest part of town. We then set a trail to the northwest toward the mountains. We turned a corner and we found ourselves in a ranch yard. We could see a trail leading out the back of the corrals, so we opened a gate and cut across somebody's yard. This was a sheep ranch a couple of miles east of McDermott. The Nouque family was up and out in the corrals, so Loyal chatted with them and told them we were headed to Star Valley. They told him we should be able to make a line shack by noon and then go on to Tent Creek by dark.

We started climbing soon, and it got steeper and prettier the farther we went. Wildflowers by the millions. Water dripping from the banks and just running all over. It was so incredibly beautiful. Sights not many people will ever get to see. The terrain started to change as it got steeper and steeper. There was a well-used trail up the side of this mesa. It was probably a trail the sheep herders had used to move their sheep to higher pastures in the summertime. After stopping to rest several times along the trail as we climbed higher and higher, we finally reached the high mesa on top.

It was sure different up here. After all that climbing we stopped to enjoy one of the most spectacular views we had experienced on the whole trip. Off to the west lay the broad and long valley where the dry Quinn River runs.

We headed out due east on what looked like it may have been an old wagon trail. Just two paths which in later times had been used by the local ranchers in their pickups.

We ate our sandwiches while we were traveling, letting the animals graze a little whenever we happened upon a little grass. Once the animals would pause from grabbing what grass was available, we would start them down the trail again.

It was nice having some place to go and knowing it'd be there when we got there. I kept thinking, this is almost too easy. The trail leading across the vast open country makes one appreciate the Creator and His wisdom in making this place.

Along about noon we were on a trail along the side of a small creek. We came around the bend in the creek and encountered our first real functional line shack. It was on Jack's Creek and it was settin' there all alone. The corrals were on the north edge of the fence and it had a loading chute. The line shack was sitting in the middle of a fenced area about an acre in size. It had a well and a drop bucket to bring the water to the ground.

The cabin was not locked and inside were several military cots with rolled mattresses. It had a kitchen table with several chairs in the middle of the room. On the south wall was a wood/propane combination kitchen range. Along the west wall was a propane refrigerator. Propane lights were placed above the doors throughout the cabin. It did have a locked room. That's where they keep the things that would "walk away," I guess. What a place to stop and spend your vacation. And mind you, we didn't even have to make reservations. We didn't spend too much time at Jack's Creek because we knew we were behind time if we wanted to make a place called Tent Creek by dark.

Well, we made Tent Creek right on time. It's a beautiful place, nice big clear creek. Loyal was in it as soon as the packs hit the ground. The pictures we took would have been good ones to send in to make him a candidate for an Ivory Soap baby.

We needed the rest and we knew the animals needed the rest after that tremendous climb out of the valley. After we had taken care of everything, we went to sleep with a belly full of hotcakes, gravy and bacon. Just after twilight the coyotes began their communication ritual across the vast prairie.

We were awakened about daylight by the damnedest noises I think I've ever heard. There were two range bulls, one with horns the other without. I don't know how long they had been fighting, probably all night. The one without horns was just across the creek from us, bloody all over. I couldn't tell how badly he was hurt, only that he was. Off to the south there were several other bulls in all stages of finalizing a pecking order (Most of us today probably have never witnessed a sure enough real range bull fight. Nature has a way of letting these critters know how it's done and when it has to be done. Eventually one will be recognized as the dominant bull and the others will go about establishing their roles down to the ones who will be outcast for the rest of their days on the range. When a rancher introduces a new bull or bulls into the herd, this process of establishing a pecking order will go on each and every time.)

I got my 9 mm out of the pack and fired it up in the air several times, and the bulls seemed to drift on out of sight. I don't think my firing the pistol had one bit of influence on the bulls, but I felt I had at least some control over the situation.

When man looks at the animals of the earth and thinks he can improve on their ways, he is just fooling himself. Yes, the bull fight was very ferocious and the blood left upon the ground seemed to be all for naught. But once a range war and pecking order has been set up it will last a long time. They say animals live by instinct alone. If those bulls had to use the reasoning that we humans use, I'm sure that Doctor Spock and Dr. Freud would still be shaking their heads.

We got ready to leave Tent Creek, probably never to see it again. It was more like a big picnic grounds than a stopover for a pack train. At least we did get a couple of pictures of Loyal taking a bath there. We didn't have breakfast there, as we were only ten miles from Star Valley, and we would have more time there to do whatever we felt like doing.

Starr Valley.

CHAPTER TWENTY-THREE

As we rode off onto the prairie, the beauty and tranquility was one of the most shocking things anyone could ever imagine. Riding through open spaces without the least bit of human existence can be somewhat frightening. One thing for sure: out here you are the boss. You have to answer for everything you do. Out here you can't say, "Just a minute, let me check in the manual." Each and every decision that was made was with the immediate environment concerned and all the decisions had to be right. If they weren't right then consider them a learning experience.

Now enough of the philosophizing, lets get on down the trail.

We were traveling down a two-lane path made by mostly pickups. The pasture grass was very sparse and there was not a sign of any trees. Off on the horizon in all directions we had no landmarks whatsoever. We knew what direction we needed to travel as we departed Tent Creek, but if the road ever disappeared we might find ourselves in a spot I suppose you might encounter in the middle of the ocean. No landmarks. Then you would have to rely on the sun for directions.

At an easy pace out here we got to really enjoy the trip. We traveled several hours not really paying much attention to the length of the trip. We knew we should be getting close to Starr Valley, but time and distance has a way of getting away from you when you have no way of knowing exactly where you are at any given moment.

Suddenly, the trail veered to the left and started down. There in front of us was this beautiful field of prairie hay. A little valley appeared that was about two miles across. This was the starting of the Little Owyhee River. It left the valley heading northeast toward the 45 Ranch where it emptied into the south fork of the Owyhee River.

A modern windmill stood majestic overlooking the valley as it belched out water into a large water tank at a corral. As we crossed the valley floor, we saw nine antelope run off heading north up the valley. There was a nearly new metal barn and a nice modern block house the other side of it, and beyond that a big old rambling rock house. Out back was a lot of antique haying machinery. You could tell they had put up hay there in the past using horses. This was the old home place, the house that our new friend Glenn Able had described very well the other day. Off to the west and up a little hill, maybe one hundred feet away, was a large pile of stones.

We were to learn later that it was a grave, complete with a hand-carved headstone, reading: "Jack Cross, February 6, 1900." He was buried there as a testimony for all who passed this way. The information on the head stone was chiseled in with a chisel and hammer. You could tell by the marks. It makes a body wonder what happened here ninety years ago. Was it Indians? Was it sickness? Was he injured? The headstone is just mute testimony to a moment in history that will remain hidden from for us forever.

The old rock house is used for storage and is crammed full of odds and ends, many of which are one of a kind antiques. There are saddles, pack saddles and machinery of all kinds, all covered with a thick layer of dust. That alone tells us how long it has been there. It's almost unbelievable. Looking out of the little brick house, I saw three antelope; and when I walked outside they didn't run. They're not afraid of me. They just stared at me as though I'm the intruder. But, boy, are they ever good eating. If Loyal had not made us lighten the load at Joe's house, I might still have my 30-30 with me. I ain't sayin' I would have used it, but the temptation was there.

Well, I'm hard at trying to capture some of the

Dinner Table.

magic that's all around us, and put it down on paper for all posterity. I'm grinning about this one because the longest thing I've ever written in my life was a letter. And I haven't written many of them of more than two or three lines.

But, like Loyal says, "I know this is a very painful chore, but, if you wasn't doing this, you'd be doing something else."

So, ho-hum. I'll quit my bitchin', count my blessings, and make the whole world happier.

This line shack is furnished just like the one we visited back on Jack's Creek. This place is stocked with all sorts of things. On the table are all the condiments that won't spoil. The cupboards were all full of packaged goods. So I fired up the propane stove and started making supper. Loyal came in and I had a plate of ravioli sitting on the table waiting for him.

Glenn Able had brought two other family members with him, his uncles Levi Able and Leonard Crutcher, and they kept us laughing all the time.

Indians at Starr Valley.

We were out at the corrals looking at the stock. Buford was lying in the sun, not a care in the world, when Leonard said to Loyal, "I haven't ridden a mule since I was a kid. Would you mind if I try?"

Loyal said, "No, I don't mind."

He woke up Buford, got him up and took him over to the water trough so Leonard could get on easy. Mind you now he had no saddle, no bridle, no nothing but his halter. Leonard got on. Nothing to hang onto, and just like in a wild west rodeo and he had a bad one in the chute, he said, "Turn him loose."

Loyal did. Buford did. And Leonard did. All at the same time. And there is poor old Leonard lying in the dirt in that old corral. Now Buford is quite a docile type of critter most of the time, but I reckon with a stranger on his back and in a new environment he decided he really didn't care to be a part of such a situation. Really it was more of a lunge and a quick pitch and he was free of this unknown object on his back.

Leonard didn't say anything about wanting to get back on Buford again.

While all this action was going on, I was looking all over for my camera. After the show was over I found it strapped around my neck. All I could think of to say was, "Somewhere back in Buford's past he must have took a dislike for Indians." I never thought of it then, only later. What a hell of a thing to say. And I thought of it many times, that evening and the next day. What a hell of a thing to say.

One thing for sure, we enjoyed their company and liked them a lot. And for whatever it's worth, I've seen a tear in Loyal's eyes when he's telling someone about it. Well, they were on their way. They were leaving in a fairly late-model four-wheel drive Ford pick up, with air-conditioning, nice soft music, and quilted seats.

"Where did we go wrong, Loyal?"

"Hell, man," he said, "I wouldn't trade this tranquility, peace and pastoral setting for anything. We've got it, and they're still looking."

And you know something, I believe him all the way. We both pitched in and washed the dishes in a big double-tub enamel sink with running water. Eat your heart out, Betty Crocker.

We had no idea of what lay ahead of us and sort of figured it might be wise to get a good night's rest, so that we'd be off to a good start come daylight.

CHAPTER TWENTY-FOUR

At the close of this day we both agreed that Loyal and I have atoned for all the wrong doings that all white men had ever done to all the Indians throughout history. For we knew that there were three Indians still laughing about sending those two white men down the West Fork of the Little Owyhee River.

It was quite evident that no one had been this way in years, and I mean many years. The tamarisk and young sapling trees were ten feet tall and the rocks that had been moved by years of floods and rain had obliterated the trail and it was next to impossible to get through.

As it says in our number one book, "So it came to pass." I think it says that in there. Anyway, it did for us. Not more than fifteen minutes into our journey down the canyon, we had two horses in the water. My mare was on top of Duke sideways, and she damn near drowned him. He would get his head up for a short while, long enough for a breath, but she was too heavy for him and back under he'd go. I knew the way she was struggling to get off him that she was beating him up something terrible. Then here came Loyal on the run. Me, after having a laryngectomy, I had absolutely no business even being around a situation like this. Had I jumped in, I would have drowned quickly. On the other hand, I couldn't holler for Loyal, so I kept buzzing for him with my vibrator and clapping my hands. I don't think he even looked at me as he went into the creek. I don't know how he did it, just plain old brute strength, I reckon. He threw or lifted my mare off, got Duke on his feet, handed me Duke's reins, took the mare's, and started down the stream to find a place to get her out.

I led Duke up the creek about a hundred feet and brought him out on an old cattle trail, then back down to where Loyal was examining the mare.

She had some wire cuts on her back legs from sliding down a collapsed fence line. He asked if I had looked at Duke yet and seemed completely relieved when I told him Duke appeared to be all right. He wasn't satisfied with one of the cuts on the mare's leg, whether or not to sew it because it was bleeding pretty heavily.

"Do you know where the Furaderm is?" he said to me.

"Yes," I said, "there's a one-pound jar right there in the saddle bag."

He got it and dabbed it on really heavy but couldn't figure a way to bind it. He figured we'd just have to check it every fifteen minutes. We stayed right there for about an hour until the animals quit trembling, the mare stopped bleeding, and they got their wind back.

Now, this is just for all of you people who may be contemplating making such a trip as we're making right now. Please take the time to do this first: set out a good cold beer and a pencil and a paper, find an easy seat in the shade, and sit and try to think of all the things that can't possibly happen; as you think of them, write them down on paper. Then think of all that won't happen even if they could; write them down too. By golly, you'd better take precautions, and be prepared for all of them, because if they can happen, they more than likely will happen.

Take my word for it. If we could have looked into the future, we would have backtracked up that canyon and found another way to go. As a matter of fact, there was an old road connecting the two ranches (the Star Valley Ranch and the 45 Ranch we're heading to). Our Indian friends at the Star Valley Ranch pointed it out to us but said it was the long way around, and down the canyon was the best way, and the shortest.

Obviously, ain't nary one of them had been down this canyon for many years. As I've said, time marches on and there had been many changes in that canyon as we soon found out. Shortly, we began to notice driftwood hanging in the brush, and it was getting brushier and brushier all the way.

Loyal said, "There must be a dam down here. This driftwood seems to be sitting higher and higher in the brush. Have you noticed?"

Well, of course I had noticed, and I said, "Let me tell you something else. My mind has been going back and forth like the head rig in a sawmill. The last time we crossed the creek, I let my mare take a swallow or two of water and I looked down in the pool to notice that every hair on my head has turned grey just since we started this canyon. Oh yeah, there's one more thing. Do you think our friends back there decided to get even with the white man and deliberately sent us on a one way trip?"

Tsk, tsk, tsk. Loyal only grinned. I believe he could have grinned down a grizzly if he had taken a notion. But I could see his mind was working on all this too.

We ran out of a trail, and there were just boulders, rock and brush. Within minutes, I was pulling the honey mule off a boulder with my rope. She was all spraddled out. She'd found out rather quickly how steel shoes don't work at all on rocks. I was trying to go easy on her, so as not to do any harm.

Loyal said, "Just pull her off. You can't hurt a mule." He was right again. She wasn't hurt unless it was her feelings, I reckon.

Loyal said, "Well, Bert, I think we better do a little figuring. We can't go back. I don't believe that we would make it. We can't go any further ahead. We ain't between a rock and a hard place. We're in the rocks and we're in the hard place. By the way," he added, "I would like very much to talk to those three Indians right about now." Then he grinned. "Your hair didn't turn grey," he said. "It's full of trail dust."

Well, " I said, "There's plenty to eat down here, prairie chickens by the hundreds, and of course their eggs, which are easy to get."

Loyal said, "Plenty of rattlers and they're good and tasty too."

Also, we had just run a doe away from her fawn. We'd had trouble getting around it but managed that okay

"Now Loyal," I said, "I reckon we could live quite awhile right here, but on the other hand I think this would be a very poor place to die. And I believe I can find a better place. Besides that, I want to see Jan again."

With that Loyal said, "I think I'll go find a way out of here. If you'll stay with the animals for a little bit, I'll go take a look a little while ahead."

So, as the song says, "Que sera, sera, whatever will be will be."

Loyal wasn't gone very long. He said, "Just lead them up here a short way and see what we got ahead of us." About a hundred yards down the creek we began to see what the trouble was. Someone had dynamited the sides of the gulch to fill it in, possibly to keep cattle from coming up. Loyal climbed to the top and took a good look, trying to find a way to get the horses and mules this far.

Off to the left Loyal could see where some animals had come up and around the end of this barrier. Loyal moseyed over to see what he could see. He then walked up the way they had gone and soon found his way back to where we were stopped. This was another of those times when we were sure glad to have a good mule with us.

Loyal swung up on Bufford and dallied up O.D. and the Honey mule. He gave Ole Buford his head and got his attention with just a nudge of his spurs and said, "Follow us up and over."

Buford just lowered his head and up we went. When we reached the steepest part Buford just sort of sat on his haunches and down we came back into the Little Owyhee river bottom. It took a while but it was a whole lot better than any of the alternatives. After we had braked and slid our way down the other side, we found a four-by-four road, a gate, and a fence that was lying on the ground. It wasn't needed anymore. Most of all, we had a place to loosen our cinches, let the animals graze, and give everybody a chance to get a drink of water. A person sure can get uptight traveling, and it's good to be alive. I should mention here that I don't think those Indians back at Starr Valley Ranch had anything to do with our bad luck. That was my nerves talking out loud (And the finger I cut open on the same fence that gashed my mare's leg).

After a brief rest Loyal began tightening the cinches and the ropes on the packs back up, when he says to me, "Hey, Bert, what did you do with the bucket?"

I replied, "It's on top of O.D.'s pack."

He answered, "No 'tain't, it's gone and the ropes are all loose and over to one side." Then he asked what we had in the bucket anyway.

Now the bucket he was talking about is a five-gallon plastic bucket. We had two of them. We had planned on filling up some flexible wine containers and putting them in the buckets to get us across the most arid places. It just added too much weight, so we just kept the buckets to store things in. How does a body remember what he put in a bucket several days ago? Well, let's see; I think it had my old black and white checkered jacket, my extra halter, hobbles and picket rope, an extra lead rope, and our coffee pot (which was unused in favor of a can that we could clean more easily).

Well," Loyal said, "You want to go back and see if you can find it."

"Hell no," I said, "I wouldn't go back looking

for it if it was full of cold beer. I think we're the luck-
iest people in the world to come out of this mess without breaking a bone on one of the animals, never mind
our own welfare." I wasn't about to go back mounted
or afoot. "No sir, not me. My momma didn't raise no
damn fool."

We flat out didn't need that bucket or anything
in it.

Soon we started seeing cattle and figured that
we had guessed it right about why the canyon was
blocked off. Along about where we were then, it was
too narrow to get by these animals. After a couple of
hours traveling we had quite a herd ahead of us. When
the place finally opened up, the cows and calves sort
of spilled out and we found a river. It was the South
Fork of the Owyhee River, and a big river it was. The
crossing was in the rapids and running deep like we
were told it would be. We'd have to be careful. There
was a D-8 Caterpillar sitting on the opposite bank and
nobody had to tell us what that was for. If someone
was to bog down in the river the D-8 would always
be there to help pull anything out.

Loyal said, "I'm glad I'm riding Buford," so
across we went.

The Owyhee River was coming from our right
to our left. There were ripples all across the stream so
we figured this was the place to ford the river. It
seemed about knee deep on the stock and other than
a few splashes we crossed without too much water.

This was the 45 Ranch, and the house and barns were only a quarter mile up the road.

Before we got there, here came a really pretty girl, maybe in her early 40s, with a couple of dogs, walking down the road. She'd spotted us coming and came out to meet us. This was Ruth Rubelt; she and her husband Jerry run the 45 Ranch, and as we walked along with her we talked for awhile.

The ranch was well kept and there we watered up. Her husband wasn't at home and she didn't know when he'd be back, but she said we'd probably meet him on further east on this trail leading out of the valley and up on the high desert.

We mentioned the fact that we had had a real rough time coming down the Little Owyhee River. Even though it was dammed up at one point it was a tributary to the main river. She seemed surprised to see anyone come down the river. She said even she and her husband had not been up the Little Owyhee in many years. We also told her about one of our storage buckets. Yes, it had to be up the river somewhere.

Fifteen miles further along, down this same road, is the YP cow camp, our destination for this evening. This YP ranch is one of the largest cattle ranches in Idaho, with headquarters in Tuscarora, Nevada We climbed up a winding narrow road from the valley floor to the front gate of the 45 Ranch. Tired after a long morning, we decided we would stop at the gate and have lunch. Another cup of peanut butter

45 Ranch Gate.

and jelly stirred together. Just to prove we had come this way we made sure we took a picture of the 45 Ranch front gate. We were well on our way to the YP cattle camp when we spotted a plume of dust in the distance, heading in our direction.

Loyal turned and shouted, "Here comes Jerry."

He was right as usual (still not psychic, just right). Hell, it couldn't have been anyone else but Jerry way out here. It took him a good ten minutes to get to where we were.

When the dust settled and he got out of the pickup, the first thing he said was, "Where the hell did you guys come from?" He just couldn't believe his eyes and wanted to know where we were heading and so on. Loyal told him we had just come from his ranch where we'd watered up and talked to his wife for a spell, and she said we would be meeting him somewhere as we made our way to the YP cow camp.

"Well," he asked, "where did you come from before that?"

Loyal said, "Paradise, California, and we're heading for Glenns Ferry, Idaho, just to take a little ride and visit Bert's brother-in-law."

We told Jerry about the Indians, and Jerry knew them all. Then loyal told him about coming down the canyon, and he was amazed that two "foreigners" as he called us could negotiate down the Little Owyhee and survive.

He just shook his head and said, "That's incredible. Hell, I've been here seven years and it was blocked off before that. They had to keep the cattle out of the alfalfa up above and that was the only way it could be done. I find it hard to believe, but since you're here I've got to."

It was quite an experience talking with Jerry.

He and his wife had lived in that country ever since they had been married. They come out of the 45 Ranch twice a year to buy their supplies and, as he put it, "to check out how the civilized folks live." We could have stayed and talked the rest of the day, but we really didn't know what we would encounter at a place called Four Corners. Jerry told us that the YP cow camp was set up there. We had asked him of ways to get across the area we now called the "Great Owyhee Desert."

He just looked at us and said, "Y'all have traveled too far to let this place get you. Just follow the main two wheel tracks at each turn and you'll come out on the other side of the Main Owyhee River.

Loyal was getting anxious to hit the road again and said we better get started so we could get to the YP cow-camp before dark, and if we did we might have supper there (We didn't know that there was a bigger surprise at camp. One of the ranchers had told us to make sure we stopped at the YP cow camp. We needed to experience Bob's cooking. That is if he was still there with the YP crew at that moment). Jerry was still telling Loyal that it was about fifteen miles to the cow camp. A large dust cloud he pointed out was the YP crew working about ten miles the other side of the cow camp and twenty-five miles from where we were.

"I just came through there," he said, "and I've got to run along too. Best of luck to you, and maybe we'll run into each other later, and I'll see if I can find your bucket." I had told him if he found the bucket he could have it and what was in it since we damn sure weren't coming back for it. However, Loyal gave him one of his business cards, so more about that later.

YP Cow Camp.

CHAPTER TWENTY-FIVE

It was Saturday evening when we rode into the YP cow camp at a place called "4 Corners." Lo and behold the whole camp was deserted. It was an eerie feeling out in the middle of nowhere with a full remuda of horses, all the vehicles, the living quarters which were tents, and the kitchen and not a soul around. The only other living thing we found was a cage with a Raven in it. This cage was located behind the kitchen trailer. We wandered around and found a small fenced area over by the privy (two-holer). We unloaded our packs and borrowed a bale of hay and scattered it for the animals.

We did go into the kitchen, just to look around. It was a large semi-trailer converted very professionally into a field kitchen. It was evident those folks were eating well. The kitchen had a commercial stove with ovens and grill, propane refrigerators and a big table in one end. On the eastern perimeter of the camp were about seven tents, teepees or whatever they are called. Strange looking accommodations for this day and age.

It was still quiet when we turned in about dark that night.

But, all Hell seemed to break loose at about 11:00 that night. Vehicles could be heard from far off as they returned. The first to approach us was Lafe. He looked like a real cowboy to us, but we soon learned they weren't called cowboys; they were "buckaroos." He wanted to make sure we were aware he was a buckaroo, not a cowboy. Never did figure that one out. He had been to the headquarters for his weekly shower and change of clothes. Of course he had been sampling just a little of the spirits also. He was really wound up and commenced to tell us what a good outfit this YP Cattle Company was.

He said they lent him the money to buy his saddle when he signed on about seven years ago. He allowed he was one of the top-hand buckaroos so he was making $450 a month. Then he told us as a matter of fact they got three days a month off and even sometimes they got ice cream out at the cow camp. What made him the proudest was as a top-hand buckaroo he didn't have to fix any fences. He also told us stories about the loneliness of a cow camp during the dead of winter, when he was alone and it was just he and the cattle to feed every day. I really believe he could have kept going all night but we had to get some sleep.

At about four o'clock in the morning noise awakened us. Horses were racing around the corrals, snorting, whinnying and being roped. The cow camp had come alive. We looked out of our bedrolls and could see cowboys or rather buckaroos scurrying every which way. They were feeding, cleaning, and then saddling their mounts, getting ready for a hard day's work on the range. There were seven or eight buckaroos and they were loading the horses into two stock trailers heading out to work some more young calves about five miles to the northeast of the cow camp.

Working Cattle on the YP.

CHAPTER TWENTY-SIX

afe had told us last night that each buckaroo was issued five to seven head of horses. Loyal's description of them went like this. "Each one of them stood about fifteen hands and weighed about 1200 pounds. Big stout horses with big feet like the original quarter horse was bred to be. Way before the racing folks started breeding in the thoroughbred blood with the spindly legs and little feet. They looked like they had just come off the 6666 Ranch in west Texas in the late 1940s."

It was way too noisy to go back to sleep, so we got up and got dressed. We could smell coffee in the distance. That kind of helped us mosey over to the kitchen trailer. The cook, who introduced himself as Bob Mohr, told us he'd get us a cup of coffee, but breakfast for us would have to wait until the working crew was loaded up and gone. Sounded okay with us.

We had been told by several folks on the trail before that if we came across the YP cow camp that Bob would see that we would be very well fed. We stepped up into the kitchen to have a look see and the food in there looked like you might find at a five star restaurant in a big city. There was a platter of bacon, a platter of sausages, a platter of eggs, stacks of hot cakes, a big bowl of gravy, and homemade light bread biscuits. On the table was a big bowl of butter and another bowl of jam. What looked like real silverware and cloth napkins were on the table. A big coffee pot was being passed around from one end to the other.

"No wonder everybody loves you, Bob," I told him. We sat down on some folding chairs outside the kitchen trailer drinking coffee as the buckaroos finished eating at the table in the kitchen.

What we experienced next, most folks will never see. Loyal said this ritual reminded him of pay day way back when he was in the military. There you would stand in a long line, then you would step before the paymaster who was usually one of the company officers and say, "Private *So and So*, reporting for pay, Sir."

After each buckaroo finished eating, he would step down out of the trailer and put on his wide-brimmed hat and step before Bob, coming to the position of attention. Each one would say the same thing, "Thanks for breakfast, Bob."

Loyal said this ritual should be practiced more in all kitchens.

After the last one of the buckaroos was on his way and the vehicles loaded with portable corrals and horses headed out, Bob said it was time for us. I'm here to tell y'all that breakfast will be remembered for quite a while. I don't know how many cups of coffee we drank as we talked and talked. Then Bob allowed he needed to get started on making and then taking the crew out a lunch. So we prepared to part company, hating to do it, but realizing it had to be done. I reckon we were saddled up and mounted by about eight o'clock.

On the trail again, we headed for the dust cloud off to the northeast of us, hoping to find the buckaroos' working area, and/or whatever else might lay in wait out yonder.

We caught up to the crew in about an hour's time. Sure enough they were already working a herd they had gathered from that area. The crew was made up of six buckaroos and a range boss.

Nathan Kelly was the range boss. Lafe had told us the night before that Nathan, the only native Indian member of the crew, was raised on the YP ranch. As a very young kid he started to buckaroo and became a very good friend of the owner's son. When the owner's son gained control of the whole show, he made Nathan his range boss.

The crew was really something to watch. They

had set up a portable corral in a "u" shaped configuration that was narrow at the opening. They had driven the cows with their calves into the portable corral. Across the opening they had backed a pickup truck into the center of the hole to work off from. Behind the pickup they had set up a propane-fired forge to heat the branding irons.

There were two men on horseback doing the roping and four men on the ground, actually two different teams. Then there was the range boss, Nathan Kelly. The men roping would ride into the herd of cows with their calves, rope a calf by its hind legs, and drag the calf up to an inner tube tied to a stake in the ground. The other end of the tube had a pegging string tied to it.

There were two of these tubes with pegging string setups, one for each side of the pickup truck. A man on the ground would dally a pegging string around the front feet of the calf. The man on horseback doing the roping would then back up and stretch the inner tube and the calf out until the calf was stretched out lying flat on the ground. One man would go to the pickup and load two vaccinating syringes. Then when the calf was flat and stretched out the buckaroo would vaccinate it once in the neck and then once in the hip. If it was a bull calf he would then sit on the calf while another buckaroo was castrating it. One buckaroo would mark each calf with his pocket knife by cutting certain portions out of its ears. Each mark and slice was designed to let later buckaroos identify their stock. Another buckaroo would take a thing that looked like a two-handled hedge trimmer and snip the horn stubs off all the calves. Just about every one of the calves would bleed profusely after this de-horning procedure, so the buckaroo would use an iron poker out of the branding fire to cauterize the bloody wound at the base of the horn.

The last thing done was the branding. On the left hip each calf was branded with the YP brand. We witnessed another thing not usually done in the plains states. Each heifer was branded on its left shoulder with the last digit of the year of its birth. Like, we were there in 1990. Each heifer branded that year would have a "0" to let the buckaroos down through the years know just how old it was. (Now folks, if you've never been around a branding, let me tell you it has to be the stinkingest thing you'll ever encounter. Hope the wind will blow the smell away.) The buckaroo who was doing the roping would then slack off and his rope that was around the hind feet would be thrown to him. Then, the front feet were undone.

If they didn't jump to their feet they were prodded up by lifting their tail, and away they'd go, back into the herd to find their mama. Remember, there were two of these inner tubes working all the time and I'll tell you, the way these guys worked together was like clockwork. It was such a delight to see such a well-trained and dedicated crew work in harmony with each other. The boss Nathan Kelly was like manure, all over the place and working harder than anybody.

Loyal said he had done this type of work one summer when he worked for the Claremont Ranch west of Englewood, Kansas. Of course he said they only had a couple of days of it and then they were through for the year.

I wanted to get in there with those buckaroos so bad, but at seventy years old I would only have been a nuisance. Oh well, can't have everything, I reckon; but it sure was interesting to watch.

Loyal took two rolls of pictures with his 35-mm camera. Though we envied them for what they were doing, we knew they envied us also and had already said that. We had another commitment to fulfill, and though we really didn't want to go, we shook hands all the way around and waved good bye. Time's a wastin', so we were on our way.

CHAPTER TWENTY-SEVEN

For a couple of guys who didn't know where they were going, we were making good time. We followed the last directions we got; then when we were out of sight we headed off on our own to the northeast. Loyal picked a spot on the far away horizon and headed for it. After a couple hours traveling, we spotted something twinkling and glittering in the sunshine and headed for it.

Before long, the modern metal building of a gas line pumping station materialized.

Arriving at the building we discovered a good gravel road leading from it, but south, not our direction. We looked around and found a sign reading "East Fork Owyhee River." It pointed in the direction we wanted to go, and there was a trail leading that way too. Away we went again. After about a mile of descending into the river bottom we found the river. Looking up the stream we could see the pipeline spanning the gorge. A mile up the stream and a hundred and fifty feet higher it looked like a major bridge you would see in a city. As we were about to start down into the river bottom, we leveled off for a while in what was some kind of park that hadn't been used in many years. A really nice sign explained all the amenities of the Owyhee River Valley. Now, the big question was, where would we cross the river? We knew we had to find a ford somewhere.

"Well," Loyal said, "wait here, I'll go have a look see." He went down the hill and up the next hill; then after a short time he came back and said, "Follow me, but hold on."

Down and down we went and finally the last hundred feet was a sliding job. Loyal was riding the big mule Buford, and to Buford that water looked so good shining in the sun, with the whole bottom of the small valley covered with grass so green it had an emerald tint. And best of all it was belly deep on the animals.

We decided this would be a good place to take a short break, so we loosened the cinches on the stock and let them graze in this belly deep grass. We were sitting on a big flat rock, eating another peanut butter and jelly sandwich.

I said to Loyal, "How many people would you say has sat on this rock and had their lunch?"

He said, "I'll bet thousands of Indians but very few white men has crossed here in the past." We took only long enough to eat our peanut butter and jelly sandwiches and to let the animals graze for awhile, thinking that it may be a long time before they see this good of pickin's.

After tightening our cinches we were in the water and heading for the trail. It was time to find out just how deep the ford was going to be. The stream split around an island and came together just down stream from where we had planned to cross. There were ripples all the way across so we figured that was about the shallowest part. Buford knew it and no matter how deep it was, we were going down there, whether we had wanted to or not, no coaxing or spurring needed this time. Like I have said over and over, this Buford mule saved our bacon many times. Now Loyal just gave him his head and he picked the best way across and without any problems we were standing on the east bank before we had time to be scared.

Speaking of Indians, we could see their handiwork from the other side of the river. We could make out some kind of a trail leading up out of the water. The trail up there was all shale. It had been cut and stacked by hand and formed a somewhat dangerous but solid path that could and probably will be used for centuries. Narrow, dangerous, call it what you will; it was certainly a whole lot better than nothing.

It was then, and is now, a means to an end. It took us a good spell getting to the top and back up on the desert floor again. We found the pipeline right away as it looked like an endless trail leading off to the northeast. Though the pipe was buried, the signs of it will be there forever. Mounds of broken lava rock and slab cover it and every mile there is a marker. Every five miles was a manifold sticking out of the ground, with its valves and gauges. Also a slanted sign with a mile marker number on it could be read from the air by an airplane.

We started out on the pipeline at mile marker 83. Now, we had been told to stay on the pipeline for eighteen miles, which should bring us out at a place called Riddle, a couple of miles from the Duck Valley Reservation and the main highway. Remember, we only had a road map of this area and it had only a swirly blue line for the river, and nothing about the pipeline on it. Well, that seemed all wrong. We went northeast on the pipeline and followed it, went along for eighteen miles and couldn't go any further. We were plum played out, but the pipeline went right on going. At marker number 101 we stopped for the night, a dry camp, when we were supposed to be in or near Riddle. Looking over the next three ridges, the pipeline was still going, with no food or water for the animals. We didn't like this situation one bit, but we figured we would be all right as long as we found water for them the next day.

Yep! Another full course peanut butter and jelly gourmet meal. It was getting dark as we made our dry camp. Not a landmark anywhere in sight . Yes, we were out in the middle of nowhere. We took extra care to hobble the stock real close and made sure that the old bell mare was tied tight. We sure didn't want them to wander off during the night. We didn't sleep at all that night and the stars lit the sky up to the point you could see off on the horizon. We wanted to get an early start the next morning. We left this spot on the pipeline just at daylight the next morning, looking to find water somewhere soon along the way

Even taking it easy, I could plainly see it was getting to Loyal.

Finally Loyal said, "We'd better get off this pipeline and head due east. I think we are paralleling the highway, which is just fine. But we've got to find food and water for these animals. I figure we can travel just one more day and that will be it. Then we're going to have more problems than we can handle."

As we would top each ridge or high spot, I could see Loyal standing up in the stirrups gazing to see if he could make anything out that might lead to water and feed. About mid-morning we finally came upon a road leading off to the northeast. Still not knowing where it went, we decided it at least would get us off this blamed pipeline. Another hour or so up the road we hit a crossroad with a sign that said, "Jack's

Creek." I want y`all to know that anything sounding like water was a big encouragement.

In a couple of miles Loyal pointed off to the south and said, "Do you see those cows. They're traveling in a single file line 'nose to tail.' That means they're headin' to water."

We crossed the trail they were traveling on. Just a short distance up the road we saw a bridge, a concrete bridge, and under the bridge was a big pool of muddy water. Four cows were standing in it. Of course they took off when they saw us.

Loyal said, "If the cows could drink it then our animals would do okay with it."

So we led them one at a time down to the edge and they would drink some and then Loyal would exchange animals until they had all drunk their fill. The water was too muddy for us to drink; all the same, Loyal was looking around and up the far bank he saw a patch of mud with water oozing out.

Loyal took his trusty Leatherman knife and started digging at the mud. Then he asked me to get him one of the tin cups from our pack. He dug until he had created a pool about the size of a wash basin. The water came out and was crystal clear. It took several seconds for the pool to fill up but we drank our fill and filled our canteens. Yes, we could almost yell "Eureka!" out loud again.

Loyal found a post driven into the ground, a Geodetic marker that said that this was Jack's Creek. The road we were on showed on the map too. Running his finger across it Loyal said, "Over here is Little Valley. There's another creek, I think it says Wickahoney Creek, and right over here is the state highway 51." Well, he had it all figured out but he was no happier than I was.

Loyal said, "If we can make it to Little Valley I think we for sure got a fighting chance. There should be feed for the animals and that's our big concern right now."

I said, "How far to this Little Valley? Does your map show that?"

"No," he said, "but I'm guessing about fifteen miles and taking it easy I think we'll make it all right."

"That's good enough for me," I said. "Let's go."

CHAPTER TWENTY-EIGHT

We made it all right. Soon we went down, down , down, and then we were in Little Valley. We had spotted what looked like a corral about a mile down on the floor of the valley and headed cross country to get a better look at it. It was exactly what we needed, a two-inch pipe with a good stream of water running into a cement trough. It was even spilling over the sides. Because the corral gate was closed there was lots of good grazing grass for the animals inside. We took the packs off and turned them loose and along about then my mind started daydreaming. I could smell coffee.

It wasn't long until we were eating a good hot meal. Man, this was living. Everything seemed to be going our way right now. The harder things become and the more worrisome, the more you appreciate the simple little things of everyday life. Little did we know at that time that this would be our last night on the desert. We knew a road was off to the east somewhere but were not sure how far. We thought we were in Little Valley, but we didn't know for sure. But with crystal clear cold water and good feed for the animals, what more could we ask?

Next morning we were up early but we still took time to make a pot of coffee. It was one of the things we had missed what with our being forced to build so many dry camps and not wanting to take time to boil coffee. After making sure everything was secured we hit the trail again. How far we would get today we didn't know. Circling out of the spring and corral area we picked up the road again and were on our way. A mile and a half across the valley there was another concrete bridge and another geographical marker. Yes, we had been on the right road. The marks told us we were at Wickahoney Creek. Sometimes being lost has its advantages. It was a big creek and clear as a bell. Looking off the edge of the bridge we could see the creek was full of trout from twelve to sixteen inches long. As clear as the stream was we could see them swimming everywhere.

I told Loyal, "Man, I'm coming back here and doing a little trout fishing, if I can drive, that is."

We got out of this valley the same way we got in; up and up we went. Finally the road leveled out and straightened up some; this part of it had been recently graded. How long has it been since we have seen a graded gravel road?

Thinking out loud Loyal asked, "How long has it been since we had seen a telephone/utility pole?"

It had been eight days. How many people today can say that they had not seen a telephone/utility pole for eight days. There sure ain't very many, I reckon. Soon we began to hear strange noises, and then in the distance I could hear something whizzing by.

I said to Loyal, "Hell, them's cars and trucks. Do you see 'em?"

He just grinned. He said he had been seeing them for a while and knew what they were. We reached the highway and the first sign we saw said Bruneau, twenty-three miles, and we knew just past there and a couple of small towns would be Glenns Ferry, Idaho.

We traveled about five miles, and Loyal stopped and waited for me to come on up alongside him. He said, "I've been thinking, why don't we stop one of these cars and you can ride in and call your brother-in-law Verd. You could let them know we're on our way."

We had told the girls when we were in McDermott that we should be hitting the Bruneau road in seven days. This was the starting of our ninth day. Loyal figured the girls would be calling Verd and Sherri, wondering if they had heard from us.

And, with a big grin he said, "You can bring me back the biggest malt and the biggest cheese hamburger they can come up with."

I told him okay but said if I had to walk back it was going to be eaten before I got to him. I was worried what I would do if Verd and Sherri didn't answer their phone. How was I going to get back to the pack train.

"Oh, hell," he said, "You can get a ride real easy as pretty as you look now (Folks, I was in the same clothes I had put on when I left Mcdermott). Any lady will give you a ride back, even if she's not coming this way. Just leave your spurs on."

We flagged down and stopped the next car. The driver said, "Sure, hop in. I'll have you there in about fifteen minutes." At ninety miles an hour, I don't think it took quite that long. When he let me out at Bruneau I was glad. After traveling some twenty days at about four or five miles an hour it was almost like riding a roller coaster all the way.

I phoned Verd and Sherri repeatedly but no one answered. Well, that sort of let me down a bit but the hamburgers were good. I reckon by that time my gums had hardened up and I was gumming my food very well. (Remember my lost dentures). I'd almost forgotten what good coffee tasted like. I was sitting there having a good time, eating and drinking and wondering what I was going to do next. Then this arm slid around my shoulders. For a minute it scared me.

Helluva place for a mugging, I'm thinking. But this arm hugged me. Then I saw it was Sherrie and Verd standing there behind me.

They sat down and clued me in on the latest happenings. They had been looking for us for three days, driving back and forth from Glenns Ferry to the Duck Lake reservation. They said it was at least a hundred and fifty miles round trip. They'd just come upon Loyal on the highway about fifteen miles south.

They had been really upset when they had seen Loyal leading my horse with an empty saddle. Sherri said she almost passed out. And she was scared Verd was going to have a heart attack. They finally got everything straightened out and turned back to try to catch up with me at a hundred miles an hour. I told them I believed them because that salesman from Boise that I rode with to town was travelin' about that fast.

They had a bite of lunch too, and I ordered the biggest and the best cheeseburger they could make along with the biggest malt they had, to take back to Loyal. I reckoned he'd earned it. Sherri got a couple of five gallon pickle buckets with lids from the people in the restaurant so we could take some water back with us. With everyone happy we hit the road again.

When I handed that cheeseburger to Loyal his eyes lighted up just like they had going down the Janesville Grade east of Wemple's cabin That was when he realized he was the only one who had teeth to eat all the goodies and the beef jerky. We spent time watering the animals and just visiting. Soon it was time to start looking for a place to spend the night and time for Verd and Sherri to shove off. Sherri was into real estate and had to at least show up for work in the morning. Verd said not to worry. He'd be back out fairly early in the morning with more hay and water and something to eat. "Don't worry about fixing anything and see you then."

CHAPTER TWENTY-NINE

The sun was just going down over the mountain off to the west when they left, so we crossed the road and found a spot about a quarter of a mile west and decided we would spend the night there. By dark we were in our bed rolls. The stock was so tired it didn't take them to long to settle in for the night. There was not much for them to eat because the pickin's for them out here were mighty thin. We were more or less on antelope grazing range, and they had all the tender shoots stripped off this buck brush. There wasn't much left for the horses and mules. But as they had been fed pretty well, we were happy for them. What they needed now was rest.

We let the sun get fairly well up before we started saddling the animals, since we were going to wait for

Verd before taking off. It wasn't long and he was there, and soon we were on the road again. We had been told that today we should be able to get a view of the Snake River. Well, that's what we're here for.

Verd took off in the pickup but said he'd keep in touch. We knew he would. Tonight would probably be our last night of sleeping under the stars. We figured that tomorrow we should be pullin' into Glenns Ferry and a good long rest for everybody.

This was a slow day. We were almost babying the animals, sort of letting them pick their own pace. We were just keeping them moving. About ten miles south of Bruneau we topped a hill and there to our north we could see the mighty Snake River. We were finally on a downhill path. We estimated by then we were about ten miles out of Bruneau, which is the junction where the road forks left to Boise or right to Glenns Ferry. After tying the animals up on the west side of the road, we crossed to the little café at Bruneau for lunch.

After a fine chicken fried steak dinner and lots more of that good coffee, we headed out on the final leg of our journey. We hoped we could complete it around noon the next day, if the good Lord's willing. On the other hand, if our animals were fresh we could probably have made it on into Glenns Ferry easily this very day. Reminds me of the old axiom: Wishing don't make it so. After we left the junction we started seeing huge vegetable farms on both sides of the highway. One farm house close to the road had people working in the yard. Loyal swung down and went to talk to them about finding a place to put up for the night. We were worried that with crops all over it might be hard to find a place. While they were talking, the green grass along the road was just right for the animals, as they needed some good green feed. That helped them along a little bit. How long had it been since they had been able to graze on long tall grass?

The fella Loyal was talking to said that he'd make a phone call, and he did. The arrangements were made and he told Loyal how to get to the place we'd be camping. This guy said he would go down and open the gate. Loyal was tickled pink and he told this fellow we'd have to travel slow.

He said, "I understand, take your time." (Just another of the kind of people I've been telling you about). The place we were going to was named Indian Cove and owned by a Mr. Wooden. It was a vacant house that was completely furnished. Across the driveway were some holding corrals. Mr. Wooden told us to make ourselves at home. Mr. Wooden had another ranch next door to this one and he lived there.

We had hardly gotten the packs off the animals when here he came back with four bales of pretty good prairie hay in his pickup. He dumped the hay bales into the corral, cut the wire and spread the hay around with his feet. He was a good friend of Verd and Sherrie's as it turned out. He said he'd go phone

Verd and tell him where we were. I'd already told Verd I'd leave my bandana, a red one, in plain sight if we had to put in somewhere. I had left it on the gate. Verd didn't have a bit of trouble finding us.

Verd and Sherrie showed up just after we had got everything settled down and our bedrolls thrown on the sofa couches. Wow! It had been a long time since we had any cushion under our bed rolls. What was even better they had brought out some fried chicken and french fries and some soda pop. Then to top that off they had brought a cold watermelon. Sherrie kept asking us when we thought we would be into Glenns Ferry, which was about eleven miles up the highway.

Loyal kept stalling her for the answer. He said something like, "Well, you know, when you're dealing with animals it's hard to set a schedule." She still insisted for an answer and finally Loyal told her, "We'll be pulling into Glenns Ferry at about 1:00 P.M." That seemed to satisfy her.

When Verd and Sherrie pulled out of the yard saying, "Good night," and, "See y'all in the morning," we were probably as peaceful as we had been since we swung up into our saddles in Paradise some four weeks ago.

I remember telling Loyal, "Loyal, you were asking me in a roundabout way a whole bunch of times, why does a man who has practically everything up and do some damn fool thing like this?"

Well, I reckon this is why. Yep, I reckon this is why. Loyal? Please pass the Grey Poupon. Thank you, sir. My dad had a saying. It's odd that I think of it now. I always thought he was talking about women, but it would apply here also. He'd said, "No matter how pretty a gift is wrapped, open it very carefully. It may be something you are not ready for." What that meant, now I will explain.

When we turned in, inside the house, it wasn't quite dark yet. Outside, the no-see-ums were swarming, and we're close to the banks of the Snake River. But there were no bugs inside, and we could still see what we were doing. We were more or less happy with the way things had gone. My sleeping bag was on the old chesterfield, and Loyal had thrown his on an old sofa couch. We went to sleep almost instantly and slept for what I judged to be a couple of hours.

Then all hell broke loose. We were both looking for flashlights, and mine went under the sofa. Loyal kept saying, "What's wrong?"

I said, "I don't know, maybe a mountain lion."

Loyal went out the door with only his boots on. I had my pants on but I could only find one boot. I never did find the flashlight, although I had lots of splinters in my fingers from looking for it. All the commotion was on account of another stud horse and the mares. It was a beauty of a horse when we could see it the next morning, and it belonged to Mr. Wooden. He had neglected to say anything about it because it was in a pasture just west of where we were put up. The stud was in with a big mare that he was to breed. Since the horse was not a fence breaker, he never thought that it would go into the river and swim around the fence, which is exactly what he and the mare did. It could never happen to anybody but us. With all the squealing, grunting, hooves landing on each other, and pounding around in the dark,

Loyal handed me a two-by-four and said, "Kill that crazy so-and-so if you can."

Well, I didn't want to kill him, but I sure did poke him in the ribs and I clubbed him as hard as I could until I had him running in a circle around us. That was at least long enough for Loyal to get our animals into the corral and tie them up, since there was no gate. Once we had them inside the corral we built a good size fire in front of where the gate had been. We started gathering scrap lumber from a pile and built a gate across the front of the corral. Then and only then did Loyal go back into the house and get dressed. He did make mention that he hoped the flying critters hadn't bit him too bad.

I can truthfully say I've never seen a night go by so fast. Before we got ready to spend the night it was gone! And here it is daylight already. I made coffee, and at least something good happened because that coffee was really fine.

Loyal said to nobody in particular, "This is the last thing we needed to have happen to us. If we weren't so close I'd say lay over. These animals just ain't in no shape to travel."

"Yep," I said, "but Verd will be here in awhile, and why can't we unload some of the weight into his pickup?"

"Nope," he said, " We've made it this far and we'll go all the way. Of course," he added, "that's up to you; it's your move."

Hell, it didn't take me long to make up my mind. No, I'll go along with him, sink or swim. I know exactly how he felt. It truly had been a long, hard trip. One to remember for the rest of our lives. Why should we louse it up now? This would be our last day of traveling and with fingers crossed we'd make it. Too many people were depending on us, including ourselves. And of course I was thinking of those we had left behind. It was a sure bet our wives were worrying themselves sick.

We had all our stuff loaded in the packs and had carried them out to the corral ready to load up there. After Loyal got the string all saddled and packed up he told me, "Start leading the pack string to the road and don't stop for nothing." He grabbed that two-by-four and commenced to swing it at the stud horse, who was determined to get to the mare. Loyal backed up all the way to the road, and he must have hit the stud horse a dozen times before I got the pack string through the gate and upon the road.

CHAPTER THIRTY

Soon Verd came along and he sure was glad we'd decided to make it today. He said the whole town was up and waiting already.

Loyal said to tell them, "We've got some very tired animals and we are not going to push them. We'll be there when we get there."

Verd left us before we crossed the Snake River just west of the little town of Hammet. We stopped at a small restaurant at what Verd called "the half way spot." We picketed the string across the street and decided we would have a good breakfast.

This was a real neat little restaurant, and after twenty-seven days on the trail with Loyal and these other animals, I can truthfully say I'd never seen more beautiful girls than these waitresses. And cute too and very nice. The service was so good, and the food too. We'd go back every day we were there, taking Verd and Sherri of course.

When we got started out again we didn't make more than a quarter of a mile. All of a sudden down went Duke. Loyal threw a foot in the air and rolled to one side to avoid being pinned under him. Loyal was really ticked off. Here we have a registered Arab supposedly bred for his endurance, and we get within sight of our goal and he gives up. After a few choice words and the toe of a pair of boots into his rib cage, Duke was convinced to get on his feet.

Loyal was somewhat cynical and with his dry humor said, "Bert, do you know those sunken-in spaces above the eyes on Arabs and Tennessee Walkers? That's where they put brains in Quarter Horses." Loyal pulled the saddle off Duke, walked him around a little, then put the saddle on Buford. Loyal swung up on Buford and we started out again. Fingers crossed? You bet.

Verd came by again and said, "Five more miles," and asked, "Can you make it?"

"Well," Loyal said, "I may have to carry them one at a time and that'll take longer; but, yes, we'll make it, one way or the other."

And then we were traveling between the Snake River and the Interstate, slowly and methodically, then up and over the freeway overpass. Oh yes, It looked like we would make it fine now. I could see the Three Island State Park at Glenns Ferry.

Loyal had ridden point most of the way and I had come along and rode drag. Today, he pulled Buford off to the side and told me to go ahead.

He said, "I'll let you go on ahead so Verd and Sherrie can say, "Here comes Bert.""

He had ridden point for almost 700 miles so I reckon he had seen a clear view of a long, long, long trail. I then swung my little mare into the point position and we continued single file on our way to the place we had been preparing for and thinking of for almost eight months.

A car pulled alongside; the passenger, a pretty lady, got out with a camera in her hand. "Do you mind?" she said, "I'm from the paper."

The car drove off. She started out behind us, then alongside, then ahead of us. She was walking backwards all the time taking pictures. I couldn't believe it; she was barefoot! That's when I began to take an interest in this girl.

"Loyal," I said, "did you notice the way that young lady was barefooted?" I just happened to mention, "I really liked that. I think she's pretty snazzy, don't you?"

He just grunted; too much on his mind, I reckoned. Could be or maybe he's just getting old. Nope, he was still thinking.

Loyal said, "You'd better hope the wind don't change. 'Cuz if she gets a whiff of us, I've got an idea this little party will break up awful suddenly ."

The woman was Laurie Black, and she was the editor of the local paper, *The Glenns Ferry Pilot.*

End of Trail.

CHAPTER THIRTY-ONE

As we crossed the city limit sign that said Glenns Ferry we could see a large group of people up ahead. A short ways further up the road we found out what was going on.

When we pulled into the Glenns Ferry Welcome Center the whole town had turned out to welcome us.

Now we finally figured out why Sherrie was so persistent in knowing when we would get into Glenns Ferry. They have an annual pageant that commemorates the crossing of the Snake River at what they call Three Island Crossing. This was where the folks coming on the Oregon trail would split, some going north into Oregon and others going southwest toward the trail we had just come over from northern California

I want you to know that Glenns Ferry really

Howdy Glenns Ferry!

showed us a good time, first meeting us at the Welcome Center in their festival garb. The police department even brought by a couple sacks of prepared horse feed. Then the Chamber of Commerce took us to dinner that night and we couldn't believe those ribeye steaks. And then the next day we were the honored guests at a town barbecue. This small town could sure show some of our big cities a thing or two. You can bet your boots on that. It makes you feel comfortable, you know what I mean. It's like putting on an old worn pair of tennis shoes.

Some of our stock had to be doctored up a bit. Loyal, with his vet experience and know-how from being around horses most of his life, took care of that. He said he was real ashamed of the way two of the animals came in, but it was either bring them in or let them loose on the desert. He said the low gullet on my saddle had rubbed and galled the withers on both the Arab and my mare.

Laurie Black stopped by later and said to pasture the animals at her place, and that's what we had been hoping for. Off to the west of her house she had about two acres of good grass. This country is known for it's alfalfa growing. It is all irrigated by the river and her patch of grass was soft from just being flood irrigated. In back of her house was a loading dock where alfalfa hay was loaded in rail cars for shipment to the East. Whenever a bale of hay had a broken wire they would leave it on the platform for whoever might want it. We had to ration the alfalfa to the stock because Loyal was concerned they might founder from overeating.

CHAPTER THIRTY-TWO

We both felt we had accomplished something many folks had only dreamed about. We had been on the trail for 27 days, crossed part of four states, rode across two significant deserts. We probably rode ground that no white man had crossed in a hundred years. Maybe never!

We had experienced some situations that only happen in the movies. Loyal said this trip was the most challenging thing both mentally and physically he had ever experienced in his lifetime. What was probably the most satisfying was people we had met along the way. It's great that there are still such good and giving folks out there who will do things for you because you are you and not because they can make something out of it. Loyal had finally fulfilled a life-long dream. When we first started talking about the trek I had no idea how much work and planning he had put into this trip. Just the fact that he came up with the animals and all the tack is quite amazing. Then he put together all the maps and tried to memorize the route and the many points of interest we would pass through.

Loyal had made previous arrangements with his cousin Wayne to come from Fiddletown, California, with a big stock trailer to haul the stock and all the saddles and tack back to the Fiddletown area. Everything went so smooth, it almost but not quite worried me. I kept telling myself my worrying days are over. We had our visit with Verd and Sherrie most of all, and almost every morning we stayed in Glenns Ferry, we went to breakfast at the little restaurant we last stopped at just after we had crossed the Snake River.

As soon as I get back home, I'm going to jump in the car and take Jan for a ride to Wemple's cabin to find my teeth. Then we'll go to the restaurant in Litchfield for a real good steak dinner with chocolate pie for dessert. Seven hundred and eighty miles of mountain and desert behind us, and no more jerky hanging off my saddle horn.

Now, please believe me, I've done the things I just outlined for you. I took my wife Jan for a ride to Wemple's cabin. I found my teeth exactly where I had left them, washed them and put them in. We drove off the mountain to Litchfield and ordered a fine steak dinner with chocolate pie and whipped cream for dessert. To make sure I didn't get left out again, I called the day before to make a reservation and ordered what we would be needing. I didn't tell Jan until afterwards. I let her worry a little bit, but didn't myself, not even a little. Bright and early the next morning, I got busy making another sack full of Jerky. Oh, it sure feels good to be home again. Hallelujah!

EPILOGUE

How many times along the trail did someone say, "You're doing something I've always wanted to do"?

Our standard comeback was, "We've always wanted to do this also." But truthfully it all starts with a dream. Men that do not dream do not accomplish anything out of the ordinary. Riding horseback across parts of four states lets a person know that dreaming is just the beginning of a dream.

When you look back on this trek we took, it makes you realize that if a person wants he can do what he wants. Yes, with difficulties, but with success also.

Many of us have tried to do extraordinary things but have failed. I found out that if you try and remember what it takes to finish a marathon race, it is not just endurance, but somewhere deep down there you must be able to come up with a whole bunch of determination. Initially the road is level and smooth and the strain is not too hard. But eventually the path becomes inclined and your stamina seems to be completely depleted. The true marathoner calls it "hitting the wall." If you can just come up with the true grit to keep going you will punch through the wall and from there on it's all downhill.

Like some old cowboy in west Texas could have said, "We just pulled our Stetsons down tight on our heads and headed straight into the wind." Yes, "We poked a hole in the wind."

ABOUT THE AUTHOR

Loyal McCammond grew up in the small town of Englewood, Kansas. Englewood was such a small community that he was almost forced to participate in all the school activities. He lettered in football, basketball, and track. But when you figure his sophomore year, there were fewer than 30 kids in high school, he had no choice. He worked during the summers bucking alfalfa bales, and after graduating he left that area to find better work.

In 1961 he enlisted in the U.S. Army. During his twenty years on active duty he was stationed many places. He spent several years in Germany, two tours of duty in Vietnam, brief assignments at Fort Gordon, GA, Fort Hood, TX, Fort Monmouth, NJ and Fort Huachuca, AZ. The last years of his Army duties were spent as an Army Recruiter stationed at Blytheville, AR. He also had assignments with the Army Security Agency and the 1st Signal Brigade.

The author's military awards include: The Bronze Star, Meritorious Service Medal with Oak Leaf

Cluster, Army Commendation Medal with two Oak Leaf Clusters, Vietnam Service Medal, Republic of Vietnam Campaign Medal with 9 Campaign Stars, Good Conduct Medal 6th Award, Gold Recruiter's Badge with 3 Sapphires and the Gold Recruiter's Ring.

The Governor of Kansas appointed McCammond to be the Sheriff of Greeley County, Kansas. There, he served there from 1985 until 1989.

During his working years, he attended several schools. With his work history and school endeavors he holds the following certificates:

Certified Licensed Social Worker, Certified Licensed Electronic Technician, Certified Licensed Fresh Water Plant Operator and Certified Licensed Law Enforcement Officer.

He has three grown children by a previous wife. He and his present wife of twenty-one years, Rose, have enjoyed traveling in an RV throughout most of the United States.

9 780984 355